CLIMBING MOUNTAINS

My 5-Stage Journey To Resilient Leadership

FUNKE ABIMBOLA

TABLE OF CONTENTS

INTRODUCTION

> *"You never know what's around the corner.*
> *It could be everything. Or it could be nothing.*
> *You keep putting one foot in front of the other, and then*
> *one day you look back and you've climbed a mountain."*
>
> *- Tom Hiddleston, British actor*

The world needs more resilient leaders.

But what does this actually mean?

And are resilient leaders made or born?

I have often heard it said that resilience is a muscle that must be exercised regularly. That being the case, I can certainly say that my journey to resilient leadership – and overall leadership success – has involved a lot of 'exercise' and has been far from easy!

I used to believe that the more senior I became as a leader, the less I would encounter racism, sexism, bias, and wrongful assumptions.

I hoped that the higher up I progressed, the easier things would become.

My hope and belief was that I would eventually reach a level of seniority where I would no longer have to constantly reassert the value that I know I bring to the table.

That I would have earned my proverbial stripes.

Sadly, in this regard, I have been proven wrong time and time again.

In fact, the reverse has proven to be the case.

As a confident Black woman who has been working in the corporate world globally for over 20 years, my experiences have shown that those from under-represented groups (however we choose to define that term) present a real and increasing threat to many from majority groups.

Over the years, I have asked myself – countless times – why this is true.

As with so many things in life, there are various factors at play.

It is certainly the case that, in some instances, the level of vitriolic opposition I have faced in my career boils down to one of four key things: fear of me (by others), resentment towards me, ignorance of my underlying 'why', and pure, unadulterated jealousy.

However, it is hard to ignore the role that cognitive dissonance plays in how we interact with each other as human beings. When we are faced with something that is simply not supposed to exist, for instance, we react in extraordinary ways.

And it would seem that confident Black women are not supposed to exist in the diaspora, least of all within the higher echelons of the global corporate world.

Yet despite the numerous challenges I have faced over the years (and continue to face today), here I am.

It has taken me quite some time to write this book, and the journey of getting it to this stage has been far from easy.

So why have I called my book 'Climbing Mountains'? I have a keynote talk of the same name which is aimed at student populations and which I have delivered to thousands of students at schools and universities all over the world.

'Climbing Mountains' was also the name I gave to my 2016 TEDx Talk.

But the impetus for me to put pen to paper came, rather fortuitously, during the first wave of the global coronavirus pandemic in early 2020. At the time, the United Kingdom went into a hard lockdown, as did much of the rest of the world. Restrictions were placed on our day-to-day freedoms, and life suddenly comprised a strange set of rules and regulations that we had to follow to both safeguard the health service and prevent the virus from spreading.

My then 17-year-old son Max and I found ourselves working remotely from home for months on end, as did many students and office-based workers across the UK.

Before long, I developed a burning desire to find a significant project to work on while at home.

So, I wrote the first draft of this book.

I secured a contract with a major publisher.

We were working towards an early 2022 launch…

But then life happened, as it so often does, derailing my plan.

A combination of serious sickness in my family and other major life challenges resulted in this book being put on the back burner.

Then, as things developed further, I decided to self-publish in order to maintain independence.

Suffice to say that it has taken me some time to write this book, and I have been asked by more people than I can count when I am going to complete it!

But, as with everything in life, the timing and circumstances have to be right.

And the time is now.

FOREWORD MESSAGE
MAX ABIMBOLA

When my mum asked me to write this foreword, I didn't really know where to start and in true university student fashion, I ended up procrastinating.

I probably did this because she set a wordcount and a deadline, so it started to feel like an assignment. As time passed though, I realised I wasn't procrastinating, I just didn't know where to start.

How do you summarise such an amazing person in so few words?

Then I remembered my Grandad.

Spoiler warning for the book, but my infinitely talented Grandad spoke German fluently, and part of the beauty of that language is how deceptively complex the words are. There are several words in the German language that describe feelings so complex and specific, that they have no direct English translation.

So I spent some time doing research, and I found one word which I think might stand the test of describing my mum.

Geborgenheit - Security

Yes, you did read that correctly, the all encapsulating word is *Geborgenheit.*

No, my mum isn't secretly a bodyguard.

This is just an example of what I mentioned, German words being more complex than they appear to be.

If you enter this word into Google Translate, you will indeed get the word 'Security' as a translation, but this couldn't be further from the true meaning. Its true meaning actually has no direct English translation, but a rough version goes a bit like this...

Geborgenheit is the sum of warmth, protection, security, trust, love, peace, closeness and comfort.

It means an atmosphere of secureness, borne out of tenderness, love, care, beauty and more.

Imagine all of those feelings described in one word – that's *Geborgenheit*!

I truly think that description is beautiful. I find it amazing how one simple word can encapsulate a feeling so complex and layered.

If you've ever felt protected by somebody, that's *Geborgenheit*.

If you've ever felt comfort in somebody's presence, that's *Geborgenheit.*

If you've ever met my mum, you've experienced *Geborgenheit*.

It's the perfect word to describe her because my mother isn't just kind, she isn't just funny, she is my *Geborgenheit*.

My security.

My trust.

My protection.

My peace.

My comfort.

She is the sum of all of these, and then some.

To put it simply she's amazing and she deserves far more than a short foreword, but a book can only have so many pages.

Ich liebe dich, mumsy!

Max Abimbola

FOREWORD MESSAGE
CHRISTINA BLACKLAWS

The first time I heard Funke speak was at a Law Society event in 2012.

She was remarkable.

She spoke with such intensity, openness, and inclusivity.

I was bowled over.

A few years later, when I was firstly an office holder, and then President of The Law Society of England and Wales, she was first on my list for my campaign to increase women in leadership in law. I reached out to Funke and, of course, she was willing to help. Working with other inspiring women, we were able to make a real, global difference culminating in a Women in Law Pledge backed by the UK Government which continues transformational change within the sector.

Funke has always been a strong driving force for diversity and inclusion in law, not just with my programme but also as a volunteer for the First 100 Years project, celebrating the history of women in law. Like so many others, I greatly valued her insights, energy and skills and have had the privilege of working alongside her now over the course of many, committed years.

I know, first hand, that Funke is the real deal, walking the talk, helping others both informally and through more formal initiatives. She is a driven mentor and educator, enabling many to reach their full potential. So, even before I read it, I knew that Funke had a lot to communicate that was helpful to others. This book is the encapsulation of all that she has learned on this journey.

And profoundly, this book is a product of her own background, history, and struggles.

Despite her enormous achievements (including a well-deserved MBE for services to diversity and inclusion) Funke has faced, and importantly, overcome enormous obstacles in her own life. Indeed, the humble person that Funke, is, despite us now being close friends, I had no idea until I read the first part of the book, just how challenging some of her experiences have been. I am certain that her searing honesty and openness in describing her story in this book will resonate with many and be genuinely supportive.

The second part of the book brings together all her insights on how to overcome obstacles and succeed, as a professional and as a human being. Resilient leadership is so crucial in today's world and this book gives readers all they need to develop the relevant skills and confidence. Indeed, Funke has such kindness for others, such wisdom and intelligence, I am completely confident that her 5-Stage Journey will benefit us all.

Christina Blacklaws

Former President of the Law Society of England and Wales

CEO, Blacklaws Consulting

PART I
SETTING THE SCENE

CHAPTER 1

IN THE BEGINNING

> *"Nigeria is not a nation. It is a mere geographical expression. There are no 'Nigerians' in the same sense as there are 'English,' 'Welsh,' or 'French.' The word 'Nigerian' is merely a distinctive appellation to distinguish those who live within the boundaries of Nigeria and those who do not."*
>
> *- Chief Obafemi Awolowo, Nigerian nationalist and statesman, first Premier of the Western Region, Nigeria*

Camp One or Camp Two?

Those of us who either claim Nigerian heritage (or who, as my son Max would say, are 'Nigeria adjacent') fall into one of two distinct camps.

If you fall into camp one, you love Nigeria, although you acknowledge that there are many things about Nigeria you do not like.

If you fall into camp two, you loathe Nigeria, and there is nothing anyone can do to convince you of its many merits.

I have observed this sharp divide across society and across friendship groups. The divide even exists within my own immediate family.

I regularly find myself reflecting on how such extremes can be possible.

Personally, I fall firmly within camp one.

I agree that Nigeria has many things fundamentally wrong with it, from our leadership (which could be so much better) to the fact that there is abject poverty across the whole country. Due to the high levels of endemic corruption – plus a wide array of other various complex factors – the country has never fully realised its potential.

Nigeria's resources are not well managed. We do not have a strong maintenance culture. Life in Nigeria can also be extremely dangerous.

Yes, the list of things that are wrong with Nigeria is long and varied.

That being said, there is a feeling I have whenever I am in Nigeria, a feeling I have never felt anywhere else in the entire world... and that feeling is best described as one of intense belonging.

Visiting Nigeria reminds me of who I am, *whose* I am, and where I come from. After any time spent in Nigeria, I always return to the United Kingdom feeling more motivated than ever before.

Nigeria gives me a fresh perspective on what is possible. It motivates me to achieve even more. And, despite the odds, I know many people who are doing well in Nigeria – without having to compromise their integrity.

I was born at the Lagos University Teaching Hospital ('LUTH') in the early 1970s into a high-achieving middle-class Nigerian family. My full name was registered on my birth certificate as Olufunke Adeola Oluwatosin Akindolie. Names have tremendous importance in Nigerian culture and the full version of my first name – *Olufunke* – means 'God has given me someone to care for.' My father remains the only person to have ever consistently addressed me by the full version of my first name; since birth, most people have called me Funke – with my mother now calling me 'Funks'.

When I was born, Lagos was the capital of Nigeria, and – despite having ceded that title to Abuja in 1991 – Lagos remains the commercial capital of Nigeria, with an estimated population of approximately 30 million in the Lagos metropolitan area alone.

As both my parents were doctors, I had a privileged upbringing. My father, Dr Frank Olufemi Akindolie, gained his medical degree from Cologne Medical School in Germany, having been awarded a British Council scholarship to study medicine there in the 1960s. Because the medical curriculum was delivered in German at the time, my father spent a year learning and mastering the German language – as well as gaining an understanding of German culture – before even starting his studies. As a result, he spoke fluent German, something that made him stand out amongst the small handful of Black students studying at Cologne University at the time. His firm grasp of German culture and history had some interesting consequences, not least of which was the fact that my father only ever bought or drove a Mercedes-Benz car, so proud was he of German cars and German engineering!

After finishing his medical studies in Cologne in the early 1970s, my father made an important decision. Rather than staying in Germany, taking up the academic position he'd been offered, he instead chose to return to a postcolonial Nigeria.

It was upon his return to Nigeria that he met my mother, Dr Sarah Omodele Akindolie (née Jadesimi) who, being several years younger than him, was still completing her medical degree at the University of Ibadan. The University of Ibadan was the first university in Nigeria and was previously one of the colleges forming a part of the University of London.

Both my parents were born in Nigeria, they are both Nigerian citizens by birth, and they both became doctors, yet – in many ways – their backgrounds could not have been more different.

Although my parents are both part of the Yoruba ethnic group in Nigeria, my father's family hailed from Ondo Town in Ondo State, whilst my mother's family are from Ijebu Ode, Ogun State. My paternal grandfather, Pa Shadrack Oluwole Akindolie (fondly known as 'Papa Ondo'), made a good living as a commercial farmer whilst my paternal grandmother, Ma Bernice Oluwamamisola Akindolie (née Adeseyoju and referred to as 'Mama Ondo'), was a commercial trader. My maternal grandfather, Bishop I.G.A. Jadesimi, was a clergyman (fondly known as 'Baba Ilesha') who became one of the most prominent postcolonial Nigerian bishops, whilst my maternal grandmother, Mrs D.A. Jadesimi (née Adesina and fondly called 'Yeye' or 'Mama Ilesha') was a teacher. Baba Ilesha gained a BA Honours degree in theology from Durham University in 1933, which places me in the third generation of university graduates on my mother's side of the family.

The significance of the Ondo/Ijebu Ode differentiation within Nigerian culture will be lost on those who are neither Nigerian nor 'Nigeria adjacent', so let me try to convey the context and its relevance.

Nigeria – A Brief History

Located on the western coast of Africa, Nigeria is a country with an estimated population of over 200 million people. This makes Nigeria the most populous country in Africa.

Like the rest of the African continent, Nigeria was carved up during the 'Scramble for Africa' – a series of events that occurred in the 1800s, commonly believed to have largely taken place following the 1884 Berlin Conference until the outbreak of the First World War in 1914.

During this period, Africa was carved up and randomly divided between seven Western European powers – Britain, France,

Germany, Belgium, Italy, Portugal, and Spain. Nigeria was created as a result of this division, meaning that an estimated 250 ethnic groups suddenly found themselves part of a single, newly created nation. Now, because of this random grouping, hundreds of languages are spoken in Nigeria – including Yoruba, Igbo, Hausa, Fula, Edo, Ibibio, and Tiv, to name but a few. As Nigeria was colonised by the British, English is also widely spoken across the country.

Nigeria gained independence from Britain in 1960, and ever since it has experienced a turbulent political history. Countless military regimes have seized power from democratically elected governments through a succession of military coup d'états, and democracy has consistently struggled to maintain a solid foothold. The complexity of the ethnic groups found within Nigeria means that claims of 'tribalism' remain ever-present in Nigerian politics, and it is unlikely that Nigeria will ever fully overcome these deeply rooted divisions.

The country experienced a prolonged and devastating civil war – from July 1967 to January 1970 – that was fought between Nigeria and the breakaway Republic of Biafra. During that period, Biafra was a partially recognised country under the leadership of General Emeka Ojukwu – a Nigerian military officer who was educated at Epsom College in England, later graduating from Oxford University before completing his military training at the Royal Military Academy, Sandhurst. When Biafra declared its independence from Nigeria in 1967, it comprised a new territory of what was formerly the Eastern Region of Nigeria.

Nigeria is extremely rich in natural resources ranging from natural gas, tin, iron ore, coal, and limestone to niobium, lead, zinc, and arable land. In 1956, oil was reportedly first discovered in the Niger Delta region of Nigeria, the delta of the Niger River located directly on the Gulf of Guinea on the Atlantic Ocean. The first oil field began production in 1958, and ever since then, a selection of oil companies have come to dominate oil production in Nigeria – including Shell, BP, Mobil, Chevron, Agip, and Elf. For a period of time, this 'oil boom' led to a period of prosperity for Nigeria as a whole.

In terms of ethnic groups, Nigeria comprises three majority groups – the Hausa-Fulani (who predominantly dwell in the north of the country), the Igbos (predominantly based in the east of Nigeria), and the Yorubas (mainly residing in the south west of the country). That being said, aside from these three majority groups, there are countless other ethnic groups of varying sizes who all have their own languages, customs, norms, and distinct beliefs. In terms of the configuration of religious beliefs, Muslims (comprising approximately 50 per cent of Nigeria's population) coexist alongside Christians (who make up an estimated 40 per cent of the population), as well as a much smaller percentage of Nigerians who practise a range of traditional religions.

Nigeria's ethnic and cultural divides, however, run deeper than this; even amongst the Yoruba people of Nigeria, there are further subdivisions which predate the Scramble for Africa and hark back to a time when there was infighting amongst the Yoruba people themselves. There is a complex history here, including the Yoruba

Civil Wars that took place in the late 18th century and early 19th century. The causes of these civil wars are widely understood to have been a result of the breakdown of the ancient, dominant Oyo Empire, which resulted in uprisings, quarrels, disagreements, and feuds amongst the provincial chiefs and noble houses at the time. It is also widely understood that these conflicts were enhanced and fuelled by a Muslim slave rebellion that was sponsored by a prominent Yoruba leader.

The complexity and nuances of Nigeria's cultural and ethnic diversity have led to many Nigerians joking about the different characteristics of each ethnic group. As I mentioned earlier, my father's side of my family is from Ondo Town, and it has been said that the Ondo people are notorious for being pompous and rather arrogant. My mother's side of the family is from Ijebu Ode, and I have heard multiple references to the Ijebu people being so careful with money that they are considered to be miserly and overly frugal.

All I will say is that, for the sake of maintaining peace and harmony across both sides of my family, I can neither confirm nor deny whether or not these generalisations are rooted in any factual representation!

My Early Childhood in Lagos

Life was great in Lagos during the 1970s; I remember having an extremely happy childhood. Being raised within a high-achieving and well-supported family set-up, I enjoyed both the benefits and the responsibilities of being the eldest child in my family.

Mine is a large Nigerian family and, within Nigerian culture, cousins are often raised together like siblings – with the dynamics amongst first, second, and even third cousins resembling those of sibling groups. Looking through several family albums over the years, the photos confirm the numerous family celebrations that took place in Lagos (and, indeed, other parts of Nigeria) throughout my early childhood.

There was a steady succession of weddings, birthdays, christenings and traditional baby-naming ceremonies, Christmases, and a myriad of other public holidays and celebrations encompassing both Christian and Muslim religions and traditions.

Although the majority of my family is Christian, many family members (especially on my father's side) are Muslim. When my paternal grandfather, Pa Shadrack Oluwole Akindolie, was born into a Muslim family, his surname was Oyeneyin. He later decided to convert to Christianity, renaming himself Akindolie (a new, made-up surname, which is my own maiden name). Similarly, Baba Ilesha (my maternal grandfather) was born into a Muslim family but converted to Christianity through the influence of his maternal uncles in Ijebu Ode, taking the name 'Isaac Gbekel'Oluwa' when he was baptised.

Because of this, I have a large number of Muslim relatives on both sides of my family, many of whom have completed the Hajj (the annual Islamic pilgrimage to Mecca, Saudi Arabia) several times, becoming Alhaji and Alhaja – the honorific titles that are bestowed upon Muslim people who have successfully completed the Hajj. As a result of this (and because of the high number of Nigerians who practise Islam), we would typically celebrate both Christian and Muslim public holidays as a family – and this remains the case with many families across Nigeria today.

As practising Christians, going to church every Sunday was non-negotiable and, for years, most of my family in Lagos attended the Chapel of the Healing Cross in LUTH, often followed by a sumptuous lunch at my cousins' (the Ogunmekans') flat on the LUTH campus whilst watching American drama series *Lou Grant* on television.

Family get-togethers were marked in a time-honoured tradition, with the children consuming bottles of cold 'minerals' (or soft drinks) – bright, luminescent orange *Fanta*, bottles of dark brown *Coca-Cola*, and emerald green bottles of *Sprite*. The adults, on the other hand, would enjoy ice-cold bottles of something a little stronger – Nigerian *Guinness* (which, it is rumoured, has a much higher alcoholic content than *Guinness* brewed elsewhere!), and *Gulder* and *Star* beer. Jollof rice and fried rice were consumed in large quantities along with spicy, assorted meat stew, well-seasoned beans (sometimes with corn kernels mixed in), 'dodo' (fried plantain), pounded yam and vegetable stew, sausage rolls, meat pies, 'puff puff' (Nigerian deep-fried doughnuts) and 'moin moin' (a delicious, savoury, steamed bean pudding). For snacks, we would enjoy crisp peanuts (known as 'ground nuts'), boiled or roasted corn, and 'chin chin' (crispy, deep-fried strips of sweet dough). Despite the fact that Nigeria is a tropical country – with average high temperatures of around 30 degrees centigrade for much of the year – we would still enjoy drinking 'tea', which could either mean actual tea such as *Lipton*, or any number of hot chocolate drinks – *Milo, Bournvita, Nescao* and *Ovaltine* to name but a few.

Television was still a relative novelty in 1970s Nigeria, in the sense that there were only a small number of television channels available at the time. As was typical of much of the world back then (and this is impossible to believe now, given the sheer volume of digital content that is available for us to consume today), television stations did not start broadcasting any shows until the late afternoon and would stop broadcasting soon after the 11 o'clock news (the 'news cap') in the evening. I remember having a regular afternoon routine of returning home from school, eating a snack, doing my homework, reading a book, and only then being allowed to turn on the television to enjoy the delights of what the NTA (Nigerian Television Authority) had to offer, including *Sesame Street, Adio Family, Cock Crow at Dawn* and *The Village Headmaster.*

Nigerian advertisements were legendary in the 1970s, with the Nigerian advertising industry doing its level best to influence its target market with catchy jingles and slogans. Nostalgia is a powerful thing, and I recently found an edited clip of some of the advertisements we were exposed to during the 1970s – including adverts for *Close Up* toothpaste, *Joy* soap, and the *Thermocool* range of refrigerators.

Playing board games and card games were other fun pastimes when I was younger, with *Monopoly, Ludo,* and the card game *Snap* being particular favourites. Watching American musical films was also extremely popular during the 1970s, and – as children within an extremely close-knit community in Ilupeju (the residential part of Lagos where my family still lives) – we were constantly in and out of each other's houses, watching *The Sound of Music* and *Chitty Chitty Bang Bang.*

Power cuts were frequent and common. The National Electric Power Authority ('NEPA'), as it was called then, was forever battling to accommodate the nation's electricity needs, and many a viewing of a popular television programme was rudely interrupted by the deathly silence that ensued whenever "NEPA took light." Whenever this happened, we would all exclaim *"NEPA!"* in an exasperated tone. During prolonged power cuts, my mother would bemoan the fact that food would spoil in the freezer as it slowly defrosted. We would make sure to keep on top of our ironing when there was electricity so that we were well-prepared and well-turned-out should NEPA strike again. This was (and still remains) simply part of life in Nigeria, and we ultimately found ourselves adapting to the unpredictable nature of NEPA. Over time, we would joke that NEPA actually stood for 'Never Expect Power Again'!

My father was always mindful of our overall wellbeing, ensuring that we enjoyed our family time together to the fullest. He stayed fit by playing tennis regularly at the Lagos Lawn Tennis Club, and it was always exciting whenever we were allowed to go to the tennis club with him – and even more so when we started having tennis lessons ourselves. Lagos had and still has a number of sports-affiliated clubs, and I have fond memories of us swimming at both the Lagos Country Club in the Ikeja part of Lagos and at the Ikoyi Club.

The 1970s was also the decade that saw Nigeria beginning to enjoy the benefits of the oil boom. One of the most notable and positive aspects of this time was a renewed sense of pride and optimism in terms of celebrating key aspects of Nigerian culture and heritage – as well as African culture in general. The National Theatre in Lagos was completed and opened in 1976, a visible representation of the intersection of Nigeria's rich cultural and artistic heritage.

Having been built over an old horse racing track in 1972, the majestic Tafawa Balewa Square (also in Lagos) became yet another symbol of a Nigeria that was looking towards a progressive, postcolonial future. The Apapa Amusement Park began operating in Lagos in 1976; my parents would take me and my younger sister there, and we would enjoy the thrills of the many rides that were available at the time.

More than anything, I still remember the intense excitement we all felt about *Festac '77*, also known by its full title of the Second World Black and African Festival of Arts and Culture. *Festac* was a month-long, landmark international festival that took place in Lagos in early 1977 and that celebrated many aspects of African culture – from religion, dance, and music to fine art, drama, and literature. Over 16,000 individuals performed at *Festac,* with 56 African nations and countries of the African Diaspora being represented.

Festac was very well organised, its dedicated marketing campaign building up the anticipation of the festival for several months before it actually happened. It truly was a spectacle that not only captivated millions of Nigerians, but also Africa as a continent – as well as a more global audience thanks to the wide array of artists who performed, including Stevie Wonder from the United States and South African star, Miriam Makeba. To give you a sense of its sheer scale, at the time, *Festac* was the largest pan-African gathering to have ever taken place.

Being a coastal city, Lagos has the advantage of being home to plentiful sandy beaches. During my early childhood, the most popular beach on the Lagos shoreline was known as the Bar Beach, a prominent stretch of sand looking out at the Atlantic Ocean. The Bar Beach was a popular spot for friends and family to enjoy during weekends and public holidays, with an array of vendors selling delicious *suya* (a traditional smoked spiced meat originating from the Hausa people) in the early evenings and well into the night. The Bar Beach was well known as being a meeting point for young lovers, and I know of several married couples who had their first date there! Rather disturbingly, however, during periods when Nigeria had a military regime, Bar Beach became a site where many convicted armed robbers and coup plotters were executed by firing squad. This was, in itself, considered to be a public spectacle, with thousands of spectators (including television cameras and print journalists) being present to watch the macabre demise of some of Nigeria's most notorious criminals on a regular basis.

Although the Nigerian education system has its origins firmly founded in its British colonial history, the curriculum also reflects important aspects of Nigerian culture and history. This blended approach was reflected in the school curriculum of my early childhood in Nigeria. At both my nursery school (Iyaniwura Nursery and Primary School, now known as Basil International School) and my primary school (Corona School, Gbagada), I benefitted from both aspects of the education system whilst gaining a solid grounding in Nigerian history.

As I come from a middle-class Nigerian family, our home life was supported by domestic staff. With both my parents working as doctors and my father devoting much of his working time to building and developing his medical clinic (which would later become the First Shadrack Hospital and Maternity Home), we needed a team of live-in staff to help maintain and support the running of our home. It is not unusual to have domestic staff forming part of Nigerian families in this way, and during the 1970s, it was common for staff to not only come from other parts of Nigeria but, more broadly, from neighbouring West African countries including Togo, Benin Republic, Côte d'Ivoire, and Cameroon.

It was also common to have family members living with us for extended periods of time. As the eldest child within his sibling group, my father had the responsibility of accommodating and supporting some of his younger siblings during their holidays while they were at university. I remember at least two of my father's younger brothers living with us at both of our family homes in Ilupeju, Lagos – as they studied at university and before they both got married.

Alongside this, I have distinct memories of my paternal grandparents travelling to Lagos from Ondo Town (considered to be a treacherous car journey of over four hours, even now) to stay with us for months at a time. During their visits, my grandparents would regularly regale us with stories about family members, both living and deceased, enriched with anecdotes depicting what life was like for them in Ondo Town when they were younger. My grandparents (and indeed my parents, aunts, and uncles) were also known for sharing the wisdom of Yoruba proverbs with us. We would listen, entranced and captivated, as they recounted Yoruba fairy tales and other stories comprising the folklore of ancient Yorubaland (known as 'alo' in the Yoruba language).

Both of my parents made a concerted and dedicated effort to keep our family bonds and relationships close, for which I remain incredibly grateful. Although most of my immediate family lived in Lagos, several close family members lived in other parts of Nigeria, including Ondo Town, Ijebu Ode, and Ibadan. My childhood was littered, therefore, with visits to all of these towns, adding to the rich tapestry of my early formative years.

Throughout all of these early experiences, I gained a solid understanding of not only who I am, but the family I come from, and it is this strong sense of identity that formed the foundation upon which I would later build my success.

Music was an important feature of our home life at the time and, during the 1970s, my parents exposed me and my siblings to an eclectic mix of musical genres. My father was a dedicated fan of jazz and jazz singers, and he had an incredible singing voice himself. It was not unusual for me to hear my father singing along loudly to Louis Armstrong, Ella Fitzgerald, Harry Belafonte, and Frank Sinatra, for example! Both my parents were ardent and devoted Stevie Wonder fans, and Stevie Wonder's *Superstition* (from his popular album *Talking Book*) was played regularly in our home, as was the music of other performers including Barbara Streisand, the Jackson Five, and Diana Ross.

In addition to this, Nigerian music was a dominant feature of my childhood years, with King Sunny Ade, Dr Victor Olaiya, Onyeka Onwenu, Sir Victor Uwaifo, and Fela Kuti's music all featuring prominently in our home. Our house was also filled with the rich chords of traditional West African highlife music, and my parents (along with various friends) would regularly frequent Fela's *Shrine* to watch Fela and his band playing live music to an enraptured audience.

Some of my more unpleasant childhood memories are of the many vaccinations we had when we were younger as part of the comprehensive child immunisation public health programme that was established across Nigeria. I come from a family of medical doctors, with many immediate and extended family members having qualified as doctors specialising in various medical fields. One of my maternal aunts – Professor Buki Ogunmekan – specialised in public health, therefore it fell upon my dear Aunty Buki to vaccinate us all.

In those days, injections were not as they are now; in 1970s Nigeria, injections were large and painful, with one particular jab resembling a metal gun with multiple spokes. I still shudder when I remember 'the gun', and my current fear of injections and needles stems from those childhood inoculations, which I found to be very traumatic.

On one occasion (and I could only have been about five years old at the time), I was so nervous about having yet another injection that I actually wet myself in the waiting area! When I then received a painful injection from my Aunty Buki – immediately after wetting myself – I was careful to warn all my friends, in all seriousness, that under no circumstances must they ever wet themselves in the waiting room… because it was inevitable that a painful injection would follow by way of punishment!

But, all in all, my early childhood in Lagos was an extremely happy one. Despite the disruptions of military coups and political unrest, we still attended school and enjoyed making friends.

Personally, I loved going to school; I loved learning and was a good student. I had respect for my parents and elders and did not want to let them or my family down. I worshipped my teachers, believing they knew everything there was to know about everything (and regularly telling my parents so too!).

I had a voracious appetite for reading books and went through a phase of devouring most of Enid Blyton's novels, including *The Famous Five* and *The Secret Seven*.

I had a solid, close circle of friends, many of whom lived within a short walking distance of our home in Ilupeju, Lagos.

I had a large, supportive family. I enjoyed being an older sibling to my sister, Omowunmi (known as 'Mo', two years my junior) and my brother, Olufemi (Femi, named after my father and six years younger than me).

It truly was a wonderful childhood.

Sadly, little did I know that my idyllic childhood was about to come to a rather abrupt end…

CHAPTER 2

MOVING TO THE UK

"Those curveballs are always coming.
Eventually, you learn to hit some of them."

- Dana Owens aka hip-hop artist, performer,
and actress, Queen Latifah

A Permanent Change to Family Life

When I was six years old, my parents made the decision to separate.

At the time, my sister, Mo, was four.

My brother, Femi, was just months old.

Although this was by far the best decision for my parents to make under the circumstances, it changed all of our lives forever.

Unusually, due to the unique set of factors that were at play at the time, my father was awarded full custody of the three of us for a period of several years, becoming a single parent overnight. As the eldest child of the family, the responsibilities suddenly placed upon me were immense, even at the young age of six.

Although I was unaware of this at the time, both my parents were navigating a complex and harrowing emotional landscape. In Nigerian culture, when a marriage goes awry, extended family members become very much involved. Emotions run extremely high. Reactionary behaviours emerge and become entrenched, often with devastating consequences. And once certain decisions have been made and specific courses of action pursued, the damage is, all too often, already done.

This was the situation we all suddenly found ourselves in, trying to rebuild some semblance of family life within an emotionally charged environment. I saw the adults in my life behaving in ways I had never experienced before, and the impact was absolutely devastating. I heard dreadful things being said, not only about each of my parents but also from family members whom I had put my faith, trust, and confidence in. Going to school was incredibly difficult because I was now different to my other friends whose parents were still very much together. And the last thing any child wants is to stand out in any way.

For me, the most harrowing aspect of the separation was how I was suddenly thrust into the position of having to look after my younger siblings emotionally – especially my younger brother, Femi. My father was working very long hours, juggling the demands of building and running a busy medical practice whilst navigating a major, fundamental change to our home and personal life. By this point, we had moved into the house my father had been building in another part of Ilupeju, Lagos. Nothing, therefore, was the same, and it was an incredibly challenging time for all of us. A series of nannies and other domestic staff were constantly coming and going, adding to the instability within our home. Family members who tried to provide support for us struggled to do so.

It was a truly terrible, destabilising time for us all.

An English Summer School

Then, in the summer of 1981 (when I was eight), our father decided that my sister and I would attend summer school in the UK. I had never been to the UK before; travelling with my mother to Dublin when I was just a few months old was the closest I'd ever been. My sister Mo had never been to the UK either. My brother Femi, who was too young to come with us, remained in Lagos.

Rather than seeing this as an exciting new adventure, we both found our father's decision difficult to comprehend – especially as we had to have our lovely long afro hair cut short because there would be no one to help us look after our hair in England. We were also going to be separated from our brother for a period of several weeks, which upset me and my sister greatly.

Despite our reluctance, before we knew it, Mo and I were flying to England as unaccompanied minors on a British Caledonian night flight from Lagos to London Gatwick, arriving in England in the early hours of the morning. I remember thinking how cold it was in England, even though it was summer! It was a big shock being collected by strangers (albeit the extremely kind and funny Aunty 'Toy' and her boyfriend) from Gatwick Airport and then facing the very long drive from Gatwick to Somerset.

My father had paid for us to attend Orchard Portman House summer school in the village of Orchard Portman, two miles south of Taunton in Somerset; this meant a drive of approximately three hours on various motorways. I remember being badly carsick and feeling really upset about this latest turn of events.

Hours later, we finally arrived at Orchard Portman House, a substantial property with a large house set within acres of landscaped grounds. The setting was absolutely beautiful and serene, and we were warmly welcomed by Uncle Colin and his family, who ran the summer school. We later found out that Aunty 'Toy' (who had picked us up from Gatwick with her boyfriend) was Uncle Colin's daughter, and we slowly started piecing together the dynamics of the family relationships that supported the running of the summer school.

Unfortunately, on our very first day, our settling-in was severely disrupted; I was absolutely terrified when Henry, an overly enthusiastic spaniel puppy, started chasing me across the lawn. Henry was just excited and being playful, but back then, I had no concept of what his behaviour meant. The idea of having dogs as pets was completely unfamiliar to me. In Nigeria, dogs were guard dogs, and we were warned to be wary of them – because being bitten by a dog could mean contracting rabies and consequently having to have a painful set of anti-rabies injections.

So, when Henry started jumping on me, I ran for my life! This just made Henry chase me all the more, barking excitedly, which of course made me run even faster as I screamed in terror. And so the cycle continued... until I fell down, badly scraping my hands and knees as I fell. Aunty Toy was horrified, as was everyone else who was watching.

By this point, I was bleeding profusely from my wounds, so I had to be taken to hospital to have them treated, and – you guessed it – to have a tetanus jab. Given my abject fear of injections, this added insult to injury and certainly did not bode well for our first day in England. My poor dad was, justifiably, alarmed when he phoned us later that evening to check we'd arrived safely, only to be told that I'd spent several hours in hospital!

The rest of our time at Orchard Portman House was, thankfully, less dramatic. The weather improved and I remember having lots of sunshine during the summer of 1981. Orchard Portman House was a proper summer school; we had a timetable of English and other lessons in the mornings, followed by a range of activities in the afternoons. There were children from all over the world attending that summer, and my sister Mo and I made friends with a number of them. There was a swimming pool, and swimming lessons became a regular afternoon pastime. We also went to the seaside a great deal, enjoying the glorious Lyme Regis and all it had to offer.

One of the highlights of our time there was going to the cinema as a large group of children and watching *For Your Eyes Only*, the latest James Bond film, which had just been released. We stayed at Orchard Portman House for the whole summer, returning to Lagos in September to resume another school year back home.

Little did we know that our stint at Orchard Portman House would be followed by a return to England the following summer to start permanently attending school in the UK. With hindsight, my father must have planned this transition strategically, first introducing me and my sister to England through summer school before making the decision to send us to England on a permanent basis.

When we resumed our schooling in Nigeria during the 1981/1982 academic year, we had no idea that it would be our final year attending school in Lagos.

In preparation for our new life in the UK, my father arranged for us to have a new nanny who taught us etiquette and how to conduct ourselves. Of course, none of this made any sense to us at the time, as we had no idea we'd be going to live in the UK; it all just seemed so disjointed and confusing.

That school year flew by, and by the summer of 1982, the three of us (me, my sister, and this time my brother too) were on a flight to England, arriving at London Gatwick once again – except, this time, we would be starting a whole new chapter of our lives.

Early Years in England

Although it might seem odd for young children to be sent abroad for schooling in this manner, this pattern was fast becoming the norm for middle-class Nigerian families. During the 1980s, Nigeria's economy was bolstered as a result of the ongoing oil boom. My father's medical practice was also doing extremely well, so he could easily afford to send us to the UK and pay for all three of us to be privately educated.

Things became much harder during the 1990s, but it would be remiss of me to deny the fact that we enjoyed a substantial amount of socio-economic privilege over a sustained period.

This time, my father had arranged for us to live with the Handcock family in Cuckfield, West Sussex. Once the three of us had arrived on the British Caledonian flight from Lagos to London Gatwick, we were picked up by a friendly taxi driver called Keith Tidy – who, it later turned out, was to be our regular taxi driver as Keith's mother, Mrs Tidy, was the Handcock's housekeeper. And, yes, the appropriateness of a housekeeper being called Mrs Tidy was certainly not lost on us at the time!

Thankfully, the drive from Gatwick to Cuckfield was much shorter than the long drive we'd had to Orchard Portman the previous summer; within 30 minutes, we had arrived at *Anderida*, the home of the Handcock family.

Mr and Mrs Handcock were a couple in their 50s who ran a thriving summer school for overseas students, right from their home. They had three children – Jeremy, the eldest (who was married and lived with his family in Wales at the time), Fiona (who was living and studying in Italy), and Tim (who was studying at university). We were the first family of children that the Handcocks had accommodated for permanent schooling in the UK and, while we were there, they would be acting as our legal guardians.

When we arrived, there were several other children in attendance at their summer school, but by the time the summer was over, it was just the three of us – me, my sister, and my brother – plus a young Egyptian girl called Niveen Esmat.

My father came to visit us that September, just before we started school. At that stage, we hadn't seen him for several months, and I remember being very upset when he left – because it suddenly dawned on us that we wouldn't see him again until the Christmas holidays.

It took us a considerable amount of time to get used to our new lives in the UK. After all, we were far away from home and everything that was familiar to us. We were also the only Black children at every single primary school we attended – St Mark's Primary School in Staplefield, Tavistock and Summerhill Prep School near Haywards Heath, Summerfold House and St Peter's School in Burgess Hill, and Lewes Old Grammar School.

With hindsight, this was an unusually large number of schools for us to be attending within a relatively short period of time, but we were navigating the British education system while trying to find a school that was a good fit for us. All of these schools were day schools and Mrs Handcock would drive us to and from school every day, unable to share the school run with Mr Handcock, who could not drive. I have fond memories of Mr Handcock faithfully helping Mrs Handcock to defrost the car in the mornings and warm up the engine before we all piled in for the school run.

School life as a Black student in the UK was strange and challenging. The three of us really stood out, which had both its benefits and its downsides. We all found the British winter to be brutal and miserable. I missed the warm humidity of Lagos and found life in England very difficult to adjust to in general. I missed home terribly and was always tearful when on the phone with my father. Plus, being the eldest child, I felt the full weight of familial responsibility, which included providing regular telephone updates to my father regarding my younger siblings' wellbeing. I also wrote to my father regularly using aerogrammes – a form of airmail at the time - which could take over a week to reach Lagos.

My father made tremendous sacrifices so he could give us the best possible education and care, and he also ensured that we spent all our school holidays in Nigeria to maintain our strong links with our Nigerian heritage and Nigerian family. Even so, I found our new way of life to be extremely lonely and challenging, especially as we wouldn't see our mother for extended periods of time. Within this context, it was impossible for me to have any appreciation of how privileged we were. In fact, I assumed that everyone attended private school. What a charmed life we had – without me even realising it!

Eventually, our school life settled down and the three of us moved from being day students to starting at boarding school. I was the first to become a full-time boarder when I started at Burgess Hill Girls School at the age of 13. By this stage, we had also left the Handcocks, had acquired a new legal guardian (the wonderful Mrs Betty Sutherland), and were being hosted by a new family, the Tibbotts. Both Mrs Sutherland and the Tibbotts lived in the village of Scaynes Hill, also in Sussex. Mrs Sutherland was a legend in Scaynes Hill, having acted as guardian to scores of Nigerian – and other overseas – students over a significant period of time. Always firm but fair, Mrs Sutherland ran an organised and strict household, instilling in us the importance of hard work and discipline.

Our time was split between Mrs Sutherland's and the Tibbotts' home. The wonderful Tibbotts welcomed me and my siblings with open arms, and I have so many happy memories of us spending half-terms and exeat weekends at Pellingbridge Farmhouse, the home of the Tibbott family. Richard and Catherine Tibbott were extremely kind to us and we became good friends with their four children – Julia, Ben, David, and Helen. We truly became a part of their family, getting to know the grandparents, uncles, aunts, cousins, and all the family pets. As a close family unit, life at the Tibbotts' closely resembled my earlier childhood in Lagos and provided the three of us with the stability we needed to thrive in the UK.

Later on, my sister Mo joined me at Burgess Hill Girls School, where we both thrived within the boarding community. My brother Femi, on the other hand, attended Streete Court Prep School in Godstone before starting at Epsom College. Despite the usual challenges of growing up – including the plethora of changes brought on by puberty – we all did well academically and socially, forming good friendships at school and immersing ourselves fully in all aspects of school life.

I have so many random recollections of those early years spent in England during the 1980s: my intense dislike of both tapioca and rice pudding, watching lots of television including numerous *Carry on* films, enjoying popular children's television shows such as *No. 73* and *Fraggle Rock,* watching *Top of the Pops* religiously and being obsessed with whatever song was number 1 in the music charts, and watching *Dallas, Dynasty,* and *The Colbys,* all lavish television series that seemed so incredibly glamorous at the time. At the age of 11, I had to start wearing glasses – a sudden and unexpected adjustment.

We discovered that we had four cousins who lived in London – Sarah, Amy, Jide, and Dipo, the children of my mother's older brother, Uncle Ladi Jadesimi, and his lovely wife, Aunty Alero. We grew up together, spending several half-terms and other holidays at my cousins' home in London – including one fateful holiday when all seven of us children caught chicken pox, much to my poor Aunty Alero's dismay! The buoyant Nigerian economy meant that both of our parents were able to visit us frequently in the UK and, consequently, we enjoyed numerous half-term breaks with both my father and my mother.

Throughout this period, we built close friendships with other Nigerian children who were also being privately educated in the UK. The bonds formed during this time remain very tight indeed and I am still good friends with many of my cohort, having spent umpteen hours flying as unaccompanied minors on British Caledonian (later acquired by British Airways) flights to and from Lagos.

Over time, as we became teenagers, we would all meet up in London for half-term and exeat weekends – and in Lagos for parties. I have many happy memories of half-term holidays spent socialising on the King's Road in Chelsea (often without my parents' knowledge… but I digress!)

My Career Choice

With both my parents being doctors who ran their own medical practices, the expectation was that I would follow suit. My father in particular made it very clear to the three of us that we were to take over the running of his hospital, First Shadracks Hospital and Maternity Home, when he reached retirement age. For years, I pretended that I wanted to become a doctor when, in fact, my aspirations lay elsewhere – I dearly wanted to become a lawyer.

Thank goodness I attended Burgess Hill Girls School, a school that really helped me out and that continues to go from strength to strength. We had great teachers and wonderful pastoral care, especially as full-time boarders. As the school was instrumental in guiding us through our teens and unlocking our unique set of gifts and talents, I have very positive memories of my time there – and, to this day, I remain in close contact with many of my school friends as well as several teachers. In fact, I often visit the school to give talks to the girls, whilst also providing support to the school in many other ways.

Elizabeth Laybourn (Miss Evans at the time, our games teacher who recently retired from being head of the school) was instrumental in recognising my sporting ability; she coached me to play netball for Sussex County for two successive seasons.

Sybil Warmisham – my French and Spanish teacher – gave me a love of languages, skilfully weaving into our lessons the many cultural aspects and nuances of life in France and Spain.

Hilary Spofforth, my chemistry teacher, unlocked my passion for chemistry and my love for – and admiration of – Madame Curie.

But it was Anne Upton who played the most pivotal role at a key stage during my time at Burgess Hill Girls School. Anne taught us history, a subject I shamefully admit I had not particularly enjoyed earlier in my schooling. She was also our head of careers, later becoming a member of the school's senior leadership team.

I will always remember the first time I met Anne.

I was 13 years old, in Year 9, and had only recently started at Burgess Hill Girls. I was one of only two new joiners that year, the rest of the Year 9 cohort having been at the school since they were in Year 7, with the majority having attended the junior school for several years prior to that. Being a new joiner meant that I was particularly curious about the teachers, asking my new classmates what they were all like.

None of their answers – or anything else – could have prepared me for the force of nature that was Anne Upton: a tall, beautiful, charismatic lady with a passion for bold leadership, history, and careers for girls.

My first history lesson with Anne was about the Wars of the Roses.

Anne's teaching style was such that not only could I vividly imagine actually being at the various battles she described, but I could also picture myself standing next to all the key figures during the 32-year series of battles between the Houses of Lancaster and York. Through her teaching, I could see the Earl of Warwick, Henry VI, Edward IV, and Richard III – all in great detail. I experienced the tension of The Battle of Bosworth Field (during which Richard III was killed) and the subsequent establishment of the House of Tudor, with Henry VII at the helm. Henry VIII and the break with Rome were similarly relayed in gripping and dramatic fashion, as was the inspiring reign of Queen Elizabeth I.

Suffice to say that history quickly became my favourite subject and was my choice of the humanities when it came to deciding my GCSE options during Year 9.

But Anne's influence went far wider than instilling in me a love of history. As head of careers, it was Anne who was instrumental in supporting my aspirations of becoming a lawyer – rather than pursuing the career in medicine that my father expected of me. Without Anne standing up for me and supporting me during the various discussions that took place around A level options and my choice of future career, I have no doubt that I would have been forced to study medicine rather than law.

When I suddenly announced that I would like to study English literature, economics, and history at A level rather than the three sciences and maths, my father was stunned, shocked, upset, and extremely worried.

Having studied medicine at Cologne University in the 1960s, my father had an extensive global medical network. He knew little, however, about the legal profession. His reaction to my announcement, therefore, came from a place of love and was driven by his fear – a fear that he would be unable to support me with a legal network, alongside his very real fear that my younger siblings would, similarly, choose not to study medicine. It was Anne who led the way in reasoning with my father, reassuring him that I would make a much better and happier lawyer than I would a doctor. As a result of this, my incredible father agreed to continue funding my further education, despite my legal aspirations having appeared like a bolt out of the blue. This was quite the turnaround, and a significant financial commitment for him given that I would be attending university as an overseas student.

I credit Anne with 'leading the charge' – together with my supportive mother and some other teachers at the school – in terms of supporting my legal aspirations. I remained in touch with Anne for years after I left school; we would meet to catch up several times a year. Very sadly, Anne died in August 2022, leaving a massive gap in my life. I owe her a debt of gratitude and cannot thank her enough for continuing to be an inspiration to me.

University Life

Burgess Hill Girls supported as many of us as were academically able to apply to Oxford and Cambridge Universities. I was academically bright and, at the time, met the requirements to secure an interview at Oxford University. I was absolutely confident that I would receive an unconditional offer from Somerville College, Oxford, as I felt that my interview had gone well. My father was also extremely hopeful, as were my teachers – including Anne. It came as a real shock, therefore, when I received a rejection from Somerville College just before Christmas of 1990; it was a significant knockback at the time, making for an utterly miserable Christmas holiday in Lagos.

However, by the time I returned to school for the second term of the 1990/1991 academic year in January, I was determined to put this disappointment behind me. I finalised my university applications and chose Newcastle University as my top choice, applying to study law.

To my delight, having attended an interview at Newcastle Law School (after which I enjoyed a fantastic night out with some of the law students on the famous Quayside!), I received a reduced offer from the law school and was excited to start at Newcastle University in September 1991.

Life in the North East was a welcome breath of fresh air after over a decade spent in Sussex in the Southern Home Counties. Up to that point, I'd had very limited exposure to others from diverse backgrounds, especially people from different socio-economic backgrounds to mine. I had never heard a Mancunian, Yorkshire, or Lancastrian accent. I had also never met anyone from Liverpool, Northern Ireland, or Scotland. Newcastle, therefore, blew me away with the sheer breadth of people I got to meet and the experiences I got to enjoy there. I quickly became an adopted Geordie and was regularly addressed as 'pet'.

As an extrovert, I threw myself into Newcastle's vibrant student social life, enjoying everything Newcastle had to offer: Monday nights dancing on the revolving dance floor at *The Boat*, Wednesday nights at *Club Africa* (later renamed *World Headquarters*), law department drinks at *The Cooperage* pub, and so much more. The '90s was the heyday of hip-hop, when it matured as a musical genre, and I was fortunate enough to watch several hip-hop legends live at venues across Newcastle – not least of which was the New York quartet, *A Tribe Called Quest,* and one of Atlanta's finest hip-hop groups, *Arrested Development.*

The law department had a great roster of social events. Alongside our Christmas dinners at Lumley Castle, we also had an annual Law Society Ball at the Civic Centre in Central Newcastle, and an array of other events organised by The Eldon Society (as the law department's society was then called). Having played competitive netball during my time at Burgess Hill Girls School, I became part of the law department's netball team. I made friends easily, soon having a wide circle of friends from all walks of life, several of whom I'm still in contact with today. I lived in all the main student areas in Newcastle too – Jesmond, Fenham, and Heaton.

As a woman of faith, I was heavily involved in the university's Christian Union, and I attended both Jesmond Parish Church and Westgate Road Baptist Church during my three years at the university. My sister, Mo, came to visit me during my first year and enjoyed the experience so much that she applied to Newcastle University to study medicine! Consequently, Mo and I overlapped during our time at the university, my final year overlapping with her first year as a medical student at Newcastle Medical School.

Social life aside, the academic side of studying law was not without its challenges. I found some of the areas of law difficult to grasp, most notably property law and trusts law. The first two years of my law degree were spent studying several core subjects, and it wasn't until the third year that I was able to focus on the corporate law subjects that truly interested me. My goal was to become a corporate lawyer, making my third year at Newcastle Law School by far my most enjoyable.

My three years at university absolutely flew by and, in the blink of an eye, we were all graduating. My mother was able to fly over from Nigeria to attend my graduation, which made it all the more special.

Following graduation, I packed up all my belongings out of my third-year accommodation and left them at the home of my dear friend, Rachael Stanfield, and her family in Jesmond. The plan was for me to spend the summer holiday in Lagos and then return to the UK to continue my postgraduate legal studies.

With this in mind – and having packed just the one suitcase – in July 1994 I boarded yet another British Airways flight bound for Lagos, saying, *"Goodbye!"* and, *"See you soon!"* to my fellow Newcastle law graduates.

CHAPTER 3

MAROONED IN LAGOS

"Life is what happens when you are busy making other plans."

- John Lennon, performer and member of The Beatles

Political Unrest and Turmoil

The summer of 1994 was fraught with intense political unrest and economic turmoil, all of which had been building upon a series of events occurring over the preceding years.

The year 1993 began with much promise and hope for democracy in Nigeria. The country was gearing up for important elections on the 12th of June, the first presidential elections in Nigeria since a previous military coup in 1983. Supported by Major General Ibrahim Badamasi Babangida (known as 'IBB', Nigeria's military ruler at the time), the elections would herald a welcome return to civilian rule in Nigeria.

Chief Moshood Abiola – a prominent and popular Yoruba Muslim businessman, publisher, and aristocrat – emerged as the apparent winner of the June 12th election for the Social Democratic Party. Displeased with this result, IBB claimed election irregularities, annulling the election result. He steadfastly refused to declare Abiola as the winner, and his actions led to nationwide protests and strikes by the oil workers unions and other organisations, sparking yet more political unrest across the country.

The annulment of the June 12th election served to entrench the ethnic divides that continue to taint Nigerian politics to this day. Ever since the country was granted independence in 1960, political power in Nigeria has been dominated by the Hausa-Fulani, one of Nigeria's three majority ethnic groups, who predominantly reside in the north of the country. The June 12th election result, with strong support for Abiola (a Yoruba Muslim from the south), would have given Nigeria's estimated 250 ethnic groups the opportunity to finally unite. Sadly, this opportunity was lost when the election results were annulled by IBB. Who knows where Nigeria would be now had those results been acknowledged?

IBB eventually resigned, leaving Nigeria to be led by an interim civilian government headed by Ernest Shonekan, a Yoruba industrialist. Amongst other things, Shonekan called for another general election in February 1994 – news that was, understandably, met with much outrage from many of those in Abiola's camp who still maintained that Abiola was the rightful winner of the June 12th election. More unrest followed that November when the government increased fuel prices by nearly 700 per cent. The

Nigeria Labour Congress called for a nationwide strike, and when the Lagos High Court declared that the interim government was illegal, the government appealed the decision.

Throughout this tumultuous period, Nigeria experienced some of its worst human rights abuses. Ethnic-based attacks became rife, with some of the worst attacks being made against the Ogoni people – a minority group residing in the oil-producing delta region of Rivers State, who bravely protested the manner in which their culture and land were being destroyed by both the military and multinational oil companies. Across the country, demonstrators were killed. Many activists and journalists were detained by the government and restrictions were placed on both freedom of expression and association. Nigerian universities were also closed down during much of 1993 due to strikes by various unions, leaving thousands of students at home or idly roaming the streets.

As has often been the way during Nigeria's history, political and civil unrest created the perfect breeding ground for yet more military rule. On the 17th of November 1993, Ernest Shonekan was forced to resign when General Sani Abacha took the reins of power, becoming Head of State following a bloodless coup.

The infamous Abacha years had begun.

★★★

When I arrived in Lagos after my graduation in July 1994, the political environment was still tense and unsettled. One month earlier, Abiola had declared himself president of the country on the eve of the first anniversary of the June 12th elections and, despite going into hiding, was eventually arrested and charged with treason. Added to this, strike action continued throughout that summer, and I remember how scarce the fuel supply was as a result of the oil workers going on strike, with a severe shortage of both petrol and diesel fuel causing long queues to form outside petrol stations. Power cuts were particularly bad during this period; we would often experience days without any electricity. The exorbitant cost of diesel, coupled with the overall impact of the fuel shortages, prevented many from operating their generators.

Yet, despite this backdrop, it was good to be back home. My family was proud of me and celebrated my having successfully graduated with a law degree. My father was particularly proud and took great pleasure in showing me off to his friends.

Lagos continued to have a buoyant social scene despite the lack of fuel, and we navigated these issues by finding ever more creative ways of getting from party A to party B! With so many of my cohort having graduated that summer, there was a general mood of celebration and excited anticipation of what the future would hold for us. All in all, we managed to enjoy our summer holiday despite the circumstances, and the months of July and August flew by.

Then, September arrived.

And it became quite clear that, whilst my younger siblings would be returning to school in the UK, I would not be joining them.

The Nigerian Economy

The Nigerian naira is the official currency of Nigeria, having replaced the British pound in 1973. At its inception, the naira-to-pound conversion rate was set at two naira to every pound. The naira has been pegged to the US dollar at various levels over the years and has been consistently devalued.

By way of comparison, in 1973, one US dollar would buy you 0.658 naira.

When my father first sent us to school in the UK in 1982, the dollar/naira exchange rate remained healthy, with one US dollar buying you 0.673 naira.

Over time, this exchange rate worsened, and two exchange rate tiers were developed – an official Central Bank of Nigeria exchange rate, and a 'black market' exchange rate.

By the summer of 1994, one dollar would buy you 22.33 naira at the official Central Bank rate and 56.80 naira on the black market.

The challenge we now faced as a family was as follows:

My father earned his money in naira, not dollars.

And, once he earned his naira, he would then have to convert that money into dollars before he could pay our fees in sterling.

This meant that the devaluation of the naira had real consequences for us as a family, as it did for countless other Nigerians.

By 1994, my father was having to source dollars on the black market, paying 56.80 naira per dollar. The cost of paying school fees for three children in the UK became exorbitant and unsustainable, more so as the naira continued to lose value year on year. It became impossible for my father to afford everything, and it was heartbreaking to watch him deny himself so many things over the years, making more and more sacrifices so he could pay our school fees.

For instance, my father never had a holiday. He worked exceptionally long hours at his hospital. He never bought himself new clothes, he never bought himself a new car. When his peers moved into bigger houses in more affluent locations, we stayed in Ilupeju. None of this was lost on us as we saw the tremendous sacrifices he made to pay our fees. Understandably, some of his siblings failed to comprehend why he was doing this at all when there were good private schools we could attend in Nigeria. Yet my father went against the grain time and again; he remained insistent that we would complete our education in the UK, despite the levels of resistance he had to battle from certain family members.

When a decision needed to be made about whose fees could be funded and whose could not, being the first to have graduated, I had to 'take one for the team'. After all, my sister and brother still needed to finish their schooling so they could graduate.

By this stage, my father had happily remarried my wonderful stepmother, Aunty Iyabo, and I suddenly had a new, much younger sister, Yewande. As the eldest child, it would have been selfish for me to insist on my father funding any postgraduate legal studies in the UK. Besides, there were no funds to pay for those studies in any event.

So, for the first time ever that September, my sister Mo and brother Femi returned to school in the UK… without me.

A Tough Adjustment

I soon discovered that living in Lagos was a very different thing from being on holiday in Lagos.

When you holiday in Lagos, you are treated like a tourist. Everyone makes an effort to show you a good time because your time in Lagos is limited.

When you live in Lagos, you are expected to get on with life and simply roll with the punches.

Since leaving Nigeria for England we had returned to Lagos for every holiday, but I hadn't actually lived in Lagos full-time since 1982, and now – at the age of 21 – I was having to adjust to doing so.

September 1994 marked the start of one of the toughest periods of adjustment I have ever experienced. I had only packed one suitcase for what I thought was going to be a regular summer holiday in Lagos; the rest of my possessions were still at my friend's house in Newcastle. Now that I found myself in Lagos for the long haul, I simply wasn't mentally prepared for such a drastic change in my life. My close friends were all based in the UK – as were my fellow

Newcastle Law School graduates who, by now, were continuing their postgraduate legal studies whilst I was stuck in Lagos.

Overnight, I had lost my anchor, my routine, and my way of life. It was a devastating time for me.

Communicating with anyone abroad was extremely difficult in the 1990s. There was no internet or Wi-Fi and international phone calls were expensive. Without social media, email, or WhatsApp, I quickly lost touch with all my friends from school and university. Many of the letters that I wrote and sent to my friends in the UK never even arrived.

For someone who had never struggled to make friends before, I now found making new friends in Lagos to be extremely challenging; when trying to connect with others, I experienced everything from a lack of empathy to intense, blatant resentment towards me.

Unfortunately, things worsened for my father financially and never recovered, causing untold strain and stress at home. My father's health began to suffer too, putting additional pressure on us all. Life became very, very difficult and, for the first time, my father's medical practice was really struggling.

The biggest challenge of all, however, was trying to work out what I would do with my time and, indeed, my life. When your entire life plan is suddenly derailed due to circumstances beyond your control, what do you do to get yourself back on track? I felt increasingly isolated and confused, as so many variables were completely outside my control. I experienced intense loneliness and my mental health deteriorated due to a lack of purpose. I was at a loss as to what my next steps would be and was fearful about what the future would hold.

This feeling of doom and gloom was worsened by the overriding climate in Nigeria itself. With the economic downturn came more crime, and violent armed robberies became the norm. Not a day went by when we didn't hear about yet another friend or family member being attacked – or, worse, being killed during a robbery. Alongside this, there was a spate of business-related assassination attempts as the business climate worsened.

If you were fortunate enough to be awarded a large commercial contract, it meant that several others had lost out and that your life was now in danger. A close friend of my father's had an attempt made on his life after he was promoted to a senior role at the bank where he worked. One of my aunts was shot and killed at home by hired assassins who, we suspect, were paid for by business rivals. The mystery of her murder has never been solved. It was an absolutely horrible time to be living in Lagos and I became increasingly afraid of what may transpire in our day-to-day lives.

Yet with every cloud, there is a silver lining.

My younger sister Yewande, who was a toddler during this period, was a ray of sunshine; she was a precocious and very outgoing toddler who caused no end of entertainment for us all around the house. As an architect and interior designer, my stepmother Aunty Iyabo worked closely with several workmen and contractors, operating out of a home office. Consequently, there was a constant buzz of activity in the house, and Yewande really enjoyed regaling us with stories about her friends at nursery and, later, school. At this point, Yewande and I became particularly close, as I had far too much time on my hands and not enough to do with it. As well as being her older sister, I am also Yewande's godmother, which has always added a special dimension to our relationship.

Throughout all this, Aunty Iyabo was tremendously supportive and gave me stellar advice as I tried to meander this latest curveball in life. Relations between my father and I were continuously strained during this period and, with hindsight, I now realise that I blamed him for the financial difficulties that led to me being unable to continue my studies abroad. There was many an occasion when poor Aunty Iyabo was hauled into yet another argument between me and my father – as, indeed, were other family members.

Suffice to say that it was a turbulent and confusing time of adjustment for us all.

When it came to my future career, I was at a loss as to what my next steps would be. Initially, I considered abandoning my legal aspirations altogether and explored becoming an accountant, speaking to a number of accountants including my cousin, Dolapo Ogunmekan. For a period of time, accountancy and a career in investment banking seemed the best way forward. Having qualified as an accountant, Dolapo was forging a successful banking career for himself, and I was very much influenced by his success. I spent time shadowing him at work and also spent time at an accounting firm.

I quickly ruled out accountancy as an option, however, when I realised how diametrically opposed law and accountancy were as disciplines. Having graduated in law, I would now have to start all over again with accountancy, learning new principles and concepts and adding even more years of study before I could join the world of work. My future went back to being uncertain and undecided, and by then, my sense of hopelessness and despair was most acute.

Rather fortuitously, one Sunday afternoon that September, we went to visit Chief Frank Odunayo Akinrele after church. Chief Akinrele was a renowned lawyer, a dear friend of my father's, and a very kind man who wanted to help in any way he could. During our conversation, we explored what my next steps could be. He agreed that, under the circumstances, accountancy was not a viable option for me and, before long, we had hatched a plan.

I would enrol at the Nigerian Law School, starting as part of the 1995 cohort the following year. As it was still only September 1994, it was agreed that I would spend the intervening months working as a legal assistant at Chief Akinrele's law firm. As we were discussing this in Chief's living room, in walked Dolapo Akinrele, one of Chief's sons and a partner at their law firm, F. O. Akinrele & Co. Dolapo greeted me warmly and assured me I'd be well looked after at the firm.

So that became the plan. And, suddenly, I had goals again – and a purpose in life.

Working at F. O. Akinrele & Co. was a godsend in so many ways. Dolapo became a good friend and mentor, as did Demola, his older brother who was also a partner at the firm. They both gave me excellent advice about do's and don'ts, not least of which included a list of the men to actively avoid dating in Lagos! Importantly, I was able to get a head start on learning aspects of Nigerian law – having only studied English law up to that stage – and this would prove vital in supporting my start at the Nigerian Law School.

Soon, I developed a consistent routine and I found myself becoming productive again, waking up at 5 AM to leave our house in Ilupeju so I could beat the rush-hour traffic during the journey to F. O. Akinrele & Co. on the other side of Lagos. I would arrive at the firm early and get a head start on the day before my colleagues arrived. Dolapo and I would then spend the morning in court, where I would shadow him as he represented our corporate clients in various cases. This was my first ever exposure to the Nigerian legal system and I found myself enthralled by the many similarities between courts in Nigeria and England.

Our afternoons were typically spent in meetings back at the firm. I was a sponge, taking it all in, continuously writing notes, doing research, and absorbing as much as I could. I asked questions, took on board every piece of feedback, and made a consistent effort to keep learning and improving. With the firm presenting much-needed solace and escapism from some of the harsh realities of life at home, I threw myself into my work.

Although I didn't know it at the time, this period of learning was pivotal to my future legal career. F. O. Akinrele & Co. was – and still remains – one of Africa's top legal firms, regularly partnering with global law firms on large corporate transactions. The firm has a stellar client list comprising large corporations and multinational organisations. The work experience I gained and the network I fostered during this time were invaluable, laying a solid foundation for the corporate lawyer I would go on to become in the future. The work was tough but I took it in my stride, realising how fortunate I was to have this opportunity at all. I worked extremely hard lest anyone accuse me of taking this opportunity for granted.

I became good friends with Dolapo and Demola and made other new friends through them too, all of which helped me adapt to living and working in Lagos. Early evenings after work were always spent at the Lagos Polo Club, which was right across the road from the firm. An avid polo player, Dolapo was a member there, and to avoid getting stuck in rush-hour traffic, we would kill some time having drinks at the Polo Club, reflecting on the vagaries of the day.

By the time Dolapo celebrated his 30th birthday in November 1994, I felt like a true Lagosian, having settled into my new life at home. With hindsight, it's remarkable to think about the many ways in which I had to adapt within such a short period of time, and how resilient I had to become. When my sister Mo and my brother Femi came to spend the Christmas holiday in Nigeria that December, they were stunned by the change in me, never imagining that I would ever adapt to life in Lagos, under the circumstances.

There were times, however, when the headiness and superficiality of Lagos society were overwhelming, even for an extrovert like me. Like many large cities, Lagos is hectic and fast-paced, noisy and boisterous. The cost of living in Lagos is exceptionally high, and – like much of the rest of Nigeria – it is full of entrepreneurs, with many full-time employees running a 'side hustle' outside their day jobs just to make ends meet. It seemed as if everyone was hustling just to survive, let alone thrive.

I myself became a small business owner; I ran a bakery business from home, making birthday cakes and cupcakes for friends, family, and other contacts. *Funke's Cakes and Bakes* quickly became a thriving business, partly funding the purchase of my first car, a small but perfectly formed Volkswagen *Beetle*. This, on top of all the early morning starts to beat traffic, meant that my working day was extremely long and tiring. I was exhausted all the time, as was my father and my stepmother. I started to find that weekends in Lagos weren't very relaxing either, with the constant round of social engagements to attend and multiple cake deliveries needing to be made to my paying customers.

Following my parents' separation and subsequent divorce, my mother had moved to Ibadan, a quiet city some two hours away from Lagos, where she had studied medicine many years prior and was now running a successful medical clinic. My mother and I had become closer over the years, and I had several aunts and other close relatives who also lived in Ibadan. Ibadan very quickly, therefore, became my haven – a place I could escape to, away from the madness of Lagos.

As the months went on, I found myself spending more and more weekends and public holidays with my mother in Ibadan, experiencing a more measured and saner pace of life. And, as fate would have it, it was during one of my many visits to Ibadan that I met a dashing young man called Toks Abimbola, who would later become my husband.

Nigerian Law School

I started studying at the Nigerian Law School in 1995, a year after graduating from Newcastle Law School. Ironically, because I'd graduated with a non-Nigerian law degree, I was classified as an overseas student, which meant having to complete an extra year to learn the foundations of Nigerian law.

Suddenly, I found myself in a class with a group of other UK law graduates who were also Nigerian and who, like me, now found themselves in Lagos after years of living and studying in England. I made good friends with several of my cohort including Ronke Ogunbufunmi, Alero Oseragbaje, Shola Awosika, Folarin Kuku, Bunmi Balogun, Fadeke Benson, and Dolores Odogwu, many of whom I still remain in close contact with today. We experienced the pain of adjusting to our Nigerian legal studies together and were all extremely supportive of one another.

Alongside our rigorous and demanding legal studies, we enjoyed great social lives – with beach parties, birthday parties, and weddings featuring prominently during this period. Throughout my time at the law school, I continued working at F. O. Akinrele & Co., attending my lectures in the morning and working at the firm in the afternoon.

By this stage, I was in a happy relationship with Toks, who would later move from Ibadan to Lagos to start his career in advertising.

Life had moved into another interesting phase and we made the most of all the opportunities we were presented with.

Our Law School experience changed dramatically once we finished our first year together as overseas students; our second year saw us joining the Nigerian law graduates, becoming part of a much larger cohort of students. Our legal studies also intensified, and stress levels were sky-high during this time. Quickly, we became acutely aware of what would be at stake if we failed those final-year exams. For me, this would mean I'd be unable to qualify as a solicitor in England via the Qualified Lawyers Transfer Test route.

I had long since decided that I wanted to return to the UK to qualify as a solicitor once I'd qualified as a lawyer in Nigeria; despite having adjusted so well to life in Lagos and Ibadan, I still found life in Nigeria to be incredibly challenging in general. My formative years had been spent in the UK and, during my tenure at law school in Nigeria, I had been able to visit friends in the UK several times – including returning to Newcastle, where my sister was now in the final stages of completing her medical degree. I missed UK life terribly and never fully acclimatised to Nigeria's rocky economic and political landscape.

Financially, things had worsened for my father, and my mother relocated to the UK to support my siblings through the remainder of their studies. Having grown closer to my mother through my multiple visits to Ibadan, I felt her absence acutely; without her, I now felt like a fish out of water in Nigeria. Passing my second-year law school exams was essential to my plan to return to the UK, and all of us – for various reasons – felt the pressure of those exams keenly.

As the pressure intensified, so did my fear that I would not pass all the exams on my first attempt, therefore scuppering all my future plans. I found studying at home to be difficult and distracting, so instead, I spent the six-week run-up to the final exams staying with a friend of my mother's on the other side of Lagos. There, I was better able to focus on my studies and dedicate the time and energy I needed to revise and prepare for our final exams. Toks' support was invaluable during this period, and he had every confidence that I would pass my final exams on my first attempt.

The exams came and went, and then I had to endure the painful wait for the results.

So convinced was I that I had failed at least one exam that I began to make contingency plans for resits.

I felt physically sick during the drive to school with Toks to collect my exam results, and even worse when I started opening the results envelope.

To my utter amazement and relief, however, I had passed! There would be no resits! Thankfully, all my close friends had passed too and we would all go on to graduate together, becoming barristers and solicitors of the Supreme Court of Nigeria.

In 1996, we attended a joyous graduation ceremony at the Nigerian Law School's premises before flying to Abuja to enrol at the Nigerian Supreme Court.

Finally, we had done it!

CHAPTER 4

A RUDE AWAKENING

> *"Instead of letting your hardships and failures discourage or exhaust you, let them inspire you. Let them make you even hungrier to succeed."*
>
> *- Michelle Obama, former US first lady*

Another Adjustment

I quickly realised I had developed a somewhat utopian view of what my return to England would be like, and – as is often the case when we have unrealistic expectations – returning to the UK after almost three years of living and studying in Nigeria was fraught with a fresh set of unanticipated challenges. The England I had left after graduating from Newcastle University in 1994 was very different to the one I returned to in early 1997, after being called to the Nigerian Bar.

Although I had visited the UK on several occasions throughout my time studying in Nigeria, I found it incredibly difficult to adjust to living in England again. By early 1997 (and due to the limited means of communication available at the time), I had lost touch with most of my friends from Newcastle University.

Everyone was forging their own path after university, trying to find their own way in the world. In many ways, being a student at university is like living in a cocoon – one that doesn't reflect real life. It is the only period of your life where you are surrounded by a huge group of people working towards one collective goal: an academic qualification. As a university student, life is fairly predictable. This is not the case as a young professional.

One of the biggest adjustments I had to make was living in London for the first time, having only ever briefly visited the capital city in the past. Navigating life in London whilst trying to find employment presented a fresh set of unforeseen challenges. First of all, I was shocked by how expensive it was to live there. Next, my hopes of securing a permanent role within the legal profession were quickly dashed as I received a long string of rejections in response to all of my job applications. My savings ran out quickly and, to keep the wolves at bay, I started applying for temporary work, setting aside my aspirations of qualifying as a solicitor in England and Wales. At this point in my life, survival was the name of the game.

It was impossible to find anywhere affordable to live in London. The Nigerian economy continued to flounder, and my father's financial situation went from bad to worse. Having relocated from Nigeria to the UK to support my siblings through the rest of their studies, my mother was also experiencing her own obstacles in adapting to life in another country. For the first time in my life, I had to stand on my own two feet – without any parental support – and it was a real shock to the system. In addition, I had spent almost three years adjusting to life in Nigeria and had made good friends in both Lagos and Ibadan. Now, it felt as if I was starting that process all over again, with only a limited support network of friends in England.

Due to our worsening financial situation, my brother Femi was forced to take a year out from his studies after finishing his A levels. Femi's gap year proved to be precarious, as throughout that year we were unsure as to whether or not he would qualify as a home student when it came to applying for medical school. Had Femi been classified as an overseas student, it would have been impossible for us to afford the fees – added to which, Femi would not qualify for any form of student financial support.

So, it was essential that he be classified as a home student – a process that took several months to resolve, during which time Femi's future medical ambitions hung in the balance. My sister Mo was also badly impacted by the financial downturn, which had worsened as she was progressing with her medical degree at Newcastle. In the blink of an eye, our close family unit was under considerable strain, and we became increasingly isolated from one another.

By sheer good fortune, Femi and I didn't find ourselves homeless in London; at various stages during this difficult period, we were housed in the homes of our cousins, the Adenegans, in East London, for which we remain eternally grateful. Finding work that was related to a future career in law remained difficult for me, however, so I spent my first year in the UK working as a sales assistant in the West End, temping and promoting new perfume launches.

Femi – who, by now, had had his home student status confirmed for a place at King's College London to study medicine the following academic year – started working at Burger King. We were both able to move into our own accommodation and, rather bizarrely (for a period of about a year), we found ourselves living in two separate bedsits in the same street in South East London – one of life's extraordinary twists. Despite our limited means at the time, we made the most of what we could afford, looking forward to our Friday night kebabs to mark the end of another working week, listening to hip-hop music, and spending our Saturdays wandering around the local shopping centre.

Adventures in Retail

During this time I worked as a temporary sales assistant in Harrods, Selfridges, Fenwick, and Dickins & Jones, encountering lots of fellow graduates amongst my fellow temps. It was a tough transition for us all and I was especially appalled by how badly some of the customers treated us as sales assistants, often taking their frustrations out on us for no apparent reason. Swearing and name-calling were not unusual; it was a real shock to the system.

On more than one occasion, I found myself randomly serving either fellow Newcastle University graduates whom I'd known during my time as an undergraduate student, or wealthy Nigerians visiting London. I found the dynamics of these encounters to be deeply humbling and somewhat surreal. How was it possible that I was in this situation, despite all my hard work? It was impossible to process and, on more than one occasion during that first year, I did wonder if I would ever realise my dream of qualifying as a corporate solicitor.

The turning point was when Diana, Princess of Wales, was tragically killed in a car accident in Paris in August 1997. In the midst of the avalanche of grief that engulfed the nation, I came to the stark realisation of just how short life really is. As a result, I redoubled my professional efforts, continuing to apply for legal industry roles with a vengeance.

By October 1997, I had started work as a law costs negotiator, a position I held for just over a year before moving into a business support role at a city law firm. Because I was already qualified as a lawyer in Nigeria, I didn't have to study the one-year Legal Practice Course and was able to take advantage of the Qualified Lawyers Transfer Test, as it was then called. This involved enrolling in a three-month course at BPP Law School; fortunately, I was finally in a position to afford the tuition fees for this intense course of study.

By the end of 1999, I had successfully completed my transfer test exams, and life seemed to be under control once more. I was now happily married to Toks, who had moved from Lagos to London and whose own career in advertising was going from strength to strength. Being extremely supportive of my goals and ambitions, Toks encouraged me to persist – and to believe in myself.

During this time I became laser-focused on my route to qualifying as a corporate solicitor in England and Wales. The legal experience I had gained during my time in Nigeria meant that the Law Society waived 18 months of my two-year training contract, meaning I only needed six months of legal experience to qualify as a solicitor. Having every hope that I would secure a paralegal role for six months, I began to visualise myself being admitted as a solicitor, proudly attending my admission ceremony at the Law Society's premises on London's Chancery Lane.

Unexpected Hurdles

I sent off over 100 covering letters and CVs without success and was stunned by how difficult it was to secure a paralegal role. What was I doing wrong? When I approached some recruitment consultants to assist me, several told me to tone down my ambitions of becoming a corporate lawyer. One recruiter advised me that "corporate law was too competitive for a Black woman" – advice I found to be absolutely devastating. He suggested that name discrimination was at play, explaining that many candidates from ethnic minority backgrounds anglicised their names in order to secure interviews.

I was stunned by this news. How could this possibly be? What hidden dynamics were at play here, and why should I have to change my name just to secure a job interview? Surely the fact that I was Black would become apparent at the interview itself?

I found these revelations impossible to process. At no point had I thought that my name would be an issue. I had never thought that being Black would be a problem. I had a good law degree from a respected Russell Group university and had graduated at the top of my class at BPP Law School. I had cross-border corporate law experience from a major Nigerian law firm and had acted for global corporate clients, including a host of household names within the oil and gas sector. My references were stellar. So how could my name and being Black be such an issue? The sense of despair and hopelessness I felt at this time is impossible to describe.

One day, during yet another discussion with Toks about my approach, he helped me to change my perspective. The world of advertising in which he worked relied heavily on pitches and brand positioning. Was there any way that we could translate a similar approach to my candidacy for paralegal roles? Before we knew it, we had hatched a plan.

I would compile a list of 150 names.

One hundred of those names would be the names of the team leaders at the top 100 corporate law firms in the country.

Fifty of those names would be the names of the heads of the legal teams within the top 50 largest companies that had in-house legal departments in the UK.

I would find their telephone numbers.

I would pick up the phone, call every single one, and 'pitch' my candidacy to them in less than one minute.

Surely, this had to work?

So, one cold morning in January 2000, I started my cold-calling campaign, methodically working my way through the list. I made phone call after phone call without success and began to feel really disheartened. It was either a case of not getting past reception (direct numbers were not widely available) or being put through to a busy senior partner who couldn't wait to get me off the phone.

Yet I persisted, because there was no other option. This approach simply had to work.

And work it did. As I made my way down the last few names on my list, I started to gain some interest in my candidacy. A part of me wonders if it was also a case of my sales pitch having improved after making over 100 phone calls by this stage! Whatever the reason, the tide had turned, and suddenly the busy lawyers I was calling were genuinely interested in me as a candidate. Incredibly, a few of them even agreed to meet me for a coffee to discuss opportunities within their teams.

Rather fortuitously, one of those busy lawyers was Diana Bromley, who was company secretary at Wembley PLC. Diana had just been about to reach out to a recruitment consultant to help in her desperate search for a paralegal and my phone call had come at just the right time; she needed urgent help and asked that I come in for an interview as soon as possible. My interview went well and I was offered the job, starting work as a legal assistant within the legal team at Wembley PLC.

This was a significant breakthrough, my long-awaited opportunity to qualify as a solicitor. I did not take this for granted and worked harder than I thought possible, travelling for two hours from East London to Wembley every day and supporting Diana with her busy workload. I gained board exposure in my early 20s and made the most of every opportunity, networking as much as I could.

Back then, Wembley PLC was the parent company of a large entertainment group. Having just sold Wembley Stadium, the group was looking to invest in new ventures. The variety of legal work was breathtaking and invaluable to me, ranging from preparing board packs for board minutes to drafting letters before action and negotiating contracts for live artists performing at Wembley Arena.

My six months flew by and, finally, I was able to qualify as a solicitor. It was a proud day indeed when Toks and my mother accompanied me as my guests to my enrolment ceremony at the Law Society in Chancery Lane.

In September 2000, I was admitted onto the roll of solicitors and was granted my certificate to practise as a solicitor in England and Wales.

At long last, my legal career had begun.

Life as a Corporate Lawyer – and then...

I spent just under a year at Wembley before moving on to two successive Central London law firms. The working hours were long and our clients were incredibly demanding but I enjoyed it, working hard and gaining as much experience as I could. Despite the gruelling demands and regular all-nighters, there was a strong sense of camaraderie amongst the junior solicitors, and we supported each other. We celebrated the completion of corporate transactions in the time-honoured tradition of having a boozy completion lunch, always accompanied by a sense of elation and euphoria.

With Toks and I now both settled in our careers, it seemed the perfect time to start our family. I got pregnant quickly and, as the months went by, we became more and more excited. My excitement turned to anxiety, however, as I started to develop some complications linked to the pregnancy. We anxiously waited out the first few months, not wanting to tell too many people that I was expecting. I was very anxious when telling my employer, as it dawned on me that I was the only junior solicitor who was pregnant at the firm.

It soon became clear to me that women lawyers planned their maternity leave more strategically than I could have possibly anticipated, waiting until they'd become partners before starting their families. I, on the other hand, was barely two years qualified when I fell pregnant. At the time, I was the only junior female solicitor within the corporate team and the only Black lawyer in the whole firm. I felt conspicuous and began to worry about the logistics of maternity leave and my return to work. This put a considerable amount of strain on me and Toks, and this – along with a number of other fundamental factors – led to us separating when I was six months pregnant. I developed medical complications and was signed off work soon afterwards. Life had thrown me yet another curveball and I was struggling to cope.

I honestly do not know how I got through that period of time. It was 2002, I was pregnant, and I had just separated from my husband. I felt deeply ashamed and isolated, and now I didn't even have work to keep my mind off things. My mental health was in tatters and, having always been a consistent woman of faith, I was now struggling with that too.

My family's support was invaluable throughout this period. My mother was now working as a psychiatrist and my sister Mo had qualified as a doctor. Femi was completing medical school and, through sheer good fortune, he spent the last three weeks of my pregnancy in a clinical placement at the same hospital where I was due to have my baby. As I look back over that fateful year, I find it nothing short of miraculous that I made it through intact, and I am so grateful to have had my family close to me.

By the end of the year I had given birth to my son, Max, starting a whole new chapter in my life.

Throughout my year-long maternity leave, I developed a network of local friends who were facing similar situations and, together, we navigated the ups and downs of motherhood. And, although Toks and I were unable to resolve our relationship issues, he remained (and continues to be) a consistent presence and support in Max's life.

Before I knew it, my maternity leave was over, and Toks and I arranged for Max to start at a private nursery so I could return to work full-time. Despite Toks offering to pay for a live-in au pair, I stubbornly insisted that I didn't need live-in help. In my mind, the way forward was clear. I would drop Max off at nursery early in the morning, get the train to work, then leave work at the end of the day and pick Max up on the way back.

It quickly became apparent that this working pattern wasn't going to be sustainable in the long term. After all, the working life of a corporate solicitor is notoriously unpredictable, and the client demands are relentless. At the time, it was impossible to maintain a flexible working arrangement, and even well-behaved babies like Max still have the occasional night when they don't sleep.

Barely a few weeks into this, I found myself chronically sleep-deprived and exhausted. Toks reminded me of his offer to pay for a live-in au pair and I willingly accepted. We placed an advert on a popular au pair website, interviewed a few candidates, and then I welcomed the wonderful Michaela Markova ('Misa') into my home.

Misa – a bright and cheerful 18-year-old woman from the Czech Republic – was a godsend. She was a natural with Max, who was just over a year old by this point, and she was invaluable in providing consistent, live-in care and support for a full year. She would help by getting Max ready in the morning so I could drop him off at nursery before I headed into the office. Misa would then cover the afternoon pick-up and after-nursery care, holding the fort until I returned from work in the evening. As Toks and I were splitting custody and care of Max at this time, Misa would move between our two homes, seamlessly adapting to both environments. There was no fuss with Misa – she just got on with it, making my transition back to work so much easier.

When she left us after a year, we were genuinely inconsolable. How could another au pair ever compare to Misa? It really did feel as if we had lost a member of our family forever.

Suffice to say that our experience with au pairs was a mixed bag – some were definitely better than others! Yes, we had some great au pairs after Misa but we certainly had some dreadful ones too, including one who (unbeknownst to her) was already a few weeks pregnant when she arrived to take care of Max.

The stories about Max's au pairs might well be the topic of my next book, so colourful were some of the experiences we endured! But I remain grateful to have had Toks' support during this time, as he paid for all the au pairs throughout the 11-year period Max needed this live-in support.

Yet, even with live-in support, it was impossible to continue working as a corporate lawyer in a Central London law firm. So, reluctantly, I eventually left London altogether to live just outside the city, finding work with a regional law firm with more manageable working hours.

This decision was hard to make and made me very angry indeed. Why was the legal profession so unforgiving? Why couldn't flexible working patterns be accommodated? Why was the profession so 'male shaped', assuming that you were able to devote upwards of 60 hours a week to work, leaving someone else to manage carer responsibilities? The equal gender split upon entry into the profession rapidly declined as you approached partnership, which remained majority male, and this pattern was replicated when it came to ethnicity.

Surely there was a better way forward to ensure diversity at all levels of the profession?

As I progressed in my career, I began to see some wider issues beyond racism and sexism. For instance, in some firms, there was an endemic culture of bullying and harassment. Gay colleagues confided in me that they were unable to 'come out' for fear of recrimination, and it was understood that you would not be promoted if you were gay. Homophobia was rife and at least one of my gay colleagues went to great lengths to hide his sexual orientation, making up a girlfriend and a whole life outside of work that didn't exist. It was a heartbreaking moment when he finally confided in me.

But the biggest challenge by far was socio-economic, with a disproportionately high number of those progressing to senior positions in law firms having either been privately educated or educated at selective grammar schools. This is a real concern when only 7% of students in the UK have the opportunity to attend private school. The vast majority are state-educated, yet this wasn't being reflected in the profession itself. This all seemed untenable to me, and somewhat incongruous within a profession that was founded upon principles of justice, equity, and fairness.

Throughout my early career, my priority was to survive. Juggling work and home life was not easy, even with live-in au pairs, Toks' ongoing support, and more manageable hours at a regional law firm. I was constantly exhausted and often found myself taking things just one day at a time, as that was the only way I could cope.

Baby Max grew into an energetic, extroverted, inquisitive toddler, eventually starting primary school – a major milestone in our family. After this, the early years began to race by in a blur. When I moved on to a second regional law firm, I remained continuously baffled by the ongoing challenges around the lack of diversity at senior levels within the legal profession.

By this point, I had worked as a corporate lawyer at four separate law firms, and at all four firms, I had been the only Black solicitor. As I became more senior, there were fewer and fewer women lawyers – and all the other issues I had previously observed still remained. It was disappointing and worrying to see.

In those early years, I did nothing but vent and complain about the unfairness of it all. Then, gradually, I started mentoring circles for women lawyers, which soon expanded to include lawyers from all different backgrounds. My work on diversity and inclusion was very much 'behind the scenes' and intentionally so; I had no desire to be a role model or to be visible. I didn't want anyone putting me on a pedestal. After all, life was challenging enough without the weight of this additional expectation.

My work on diversity and inclusion would have remained behind the scenes but for the fact that, at the start of 2012, I secured a senior role within the UK in-house legal team of the world's largest biotech company.

Consequently, I was – literally – thrust into the limelight overnight. This was a significant job appointment within the pharmaceutical industry and, in one fell swoop, I became the most senior Black lawyer working within the UK's legal profession. The legal press reached out to me in droves and I was suddenly inundated with interview requests. I was asked for my opinion on diversity within the legal profession and was looked to for solutions.

I found it difficult to acclimatise to the sudden attention, intense scrutiny, and level of expectation that came with it. In fact, it took me several years to get used to being 'front of stage', and it remains a work in progress even today. To suddenly have your every move studied and commented upon is far from easy, especially when people are so quick to draw their own conclusions and make assumptions, both positive and negative. It was a tough transition and one that I neither sought nor wanted.

Yet, I had to make an early decision as to how best to manage my new platform and, before long, I decided to use my platform as a way to not only raise awareness of the challenges around diversity and inclusion in the legal profession, but to play my part in becoming part of the solution.

Over the years, it has become clear that this work is my calling.

For more than 20 years, I have volunteered my time towards improving equitable outcomes for others, building a large body of work focused on both social and corporate diversity. I have driven unparalleled change across the legal profession and beyond, and it has been humbling to have the impact of my work recognised. Doing this work, however, remains fraught with challenges, and the need to regularly review and assess the direction of travel.

My day job now focuses on corporate diversity, driving positive change across organisations at scale, and central to my success has been resilient leadership – the ability to bounce back from setbacks and challenges, dust myself off, learn valuable lessons, and move on.

So, let's explore my 5-stage journey to resilient leadership.

PART II
MY 5-STAGE JOURNEY TO
RESILIENT LEADERSHIP

CHAPTER 5

STAGE 1 – FOCUS

> *"One of the lessons that I grew up with was to always stay true to yourself and never let what somebody says distract you from your goals."*
>
> *- Michelle Obama, former US first lady*

As I look back over my journey to becoming the resilient leader I am today, I can see that the first stage I had to master was the ability to remain focused – no matter what.

Maintaining your focus is becoming increasingly difficult to achieve in today's busy, hectic modern world. Before writing his book, 'Stolen Focus: Why You Can't Pay Attention', best-selling author Johann Hari embarked on a three-year journey to research and explore why our attention span and ability to focus have become so severely impaired. His research was very revealing.

It confirmed that, on average, teenage children focus on a single task for only 65 seconds and that, on average, office workers can manage to focus on a task for three minutes. Multitasking is a myth. When we 'multitask', what we're actually doing is just switching from one thing to the next – and struggling to focus on any one thing particularly well.

Johann Hari's important book helped me to understand just how distracting interruptions can be when we're focusing on detailed work. A University of Oregon study by Professor Michael Posner discovered that when we're interrupted, it takes – on average – 23 minutes for us to return to the same level of focus.

No wonder I get so irritated whenever I'm interrupted!

Johann Hari's disturbing conclusion was as follows:

Far from being a personal flaw, our inability to pay attention and focus as we used to is down to a number of powerful forces, many of which are linked to the advent of technology and its impact on our lives.

Our attention and focus are being stolen on a daily basis, and it is impacting young people more than ever before.

A Personal Example

One of the best examples I've seen in my own life is what I observed with my son, Max. Max is an outgoing young man and very extroverted. Throughout his school years, his father Toks and I attended countless parents' evenings, and we were repeatedly told that Max struggled with staying focused in class. This lack of focus was severely affecting the quality of his schoolwork and meant that our exceptionally bright son was not achieving his full potential.

Our parental journey in supporting Max's ability to focus on the right things was far from easy. We went through a process of exploring whether or not Max was neurodivergent – which proved not to be the case – and his lack of focus remained a real problem for a significant number of years when he was younger.

Then, we reached a turning point. We realised that Max clearly had the ability to focus on what was important to him and, similarly, was able to ignore the things that he chose not to prioritise – because he found them uninteresting and unimportant! This became all the more evident when Max discovered his love of all things tech, including coding. Suddenly, our easily distracted son was able to spend hours on end coding and learning new programming languages.

Then, at the age of 13, he decided to build his own computer, spending all his birthday and Christmas money on ordering various parts. We watched in amazement as Max spent hours not only planning how to build the computer but also actually building it. Once he was done, he switched the computer on and it worked! Clearly, this mattered to him so he was able to make it a priority; he'd developed a laser focus on achieving his end goal.

When I posted on Facebook, mentioning the fact that Max had built his own computer, a close friend who worked at Google sent me a private message, offering Max some work experience within

Google's software engineering team in London. Max was 15 at the time, and that one visit to Google was all he needed to realise what was at stake if he remained unfocused and failed to maximise his potential.

At the heart of this was Max needing to understand his 'why' and what was motivating him. Consequently, his academic work began to turn around and he was able to focus on reaching his full potential, excelling across all his subjects and thriving in all aspects of his school life.

Your Why, What, And How

Knowing your 'why' is the key to staying focused as a resilient leader. Recognising what gets you up in the morning is critical.

Have you been able to articulate your 'why'? If not, do it now! Grab a pen and a piece of paper and write down everything that comes to mind regarding your 'why'. Then, narrow your 'why' statement down into a few short, clear sentences. I was able to articulate my 'why' when I went through this very exercise a few years ago:

My 'why' is to level the playing field by supporting others in maximising their potential.

Over the years, I've realised that there are two other things to articulate once you know your 'why': your 'what' and your 'how'. What do you need to do to achieve your why and how are you going to achieve it? I call this my 'Why, What, How' methodology and I regularly use this as a tool to help me remain focused as a resilient leader.

My 'why', my 'what', and my 'how' have developed continuously over the years and you'll find that yours will too. When I was practising as a corporate lawyer within several law firms, my 'why', 'what', and 'how' were exclusively focused on the legal profession itself. This changed as my career developed and broadened to include the pharmaceutical industry when I started working for a large biotech company. I recently fine-tuned my 'why', 'what', and 'how' further when I left legal practice altogether and started focusing on corporate diversity work within my full-time paid employment, dedicating my voluntary work time to social diversity initiatives outside my day job.

Keeping my 'why', 'what', and 'how' front of mind also helps me to know what filter to apply whenever I need to prioritise what to devote my time and energy to.

The Importance Of Boundaries

Our time is our most valuable resource, and we only have a finite amount of it available.

Making the best use of our time involves setting healthy boundaries, and the ability to say 'no' is a key part of committing to your 'why' and maintaining focus.

As I'm constantly asked to do far more than I possibly can on a daily basis, not everything I'm asked to do can be a priority. As a result, I have learnt that 'no' is a complete sentence, and being able to say 'no' unapologetically – without feeling guilty or being emotionally blackmailed into saying 'yes' – is key.

Strangely, living through the global pandemic really helped me to recognise the critical role that setting healthy boundaries plays in helping me maintain focus. With the shifting sands that we experienced throughout the pandemic and the repeated lockdowns, we were expected to pivot and adapt to the 'new normal' on a daily basis. Self-discipline, self-motivation, and emotional regulation became essential components required to maintain focus and, for me, this often meant choosing to focus on specific tasks even when I didn't feel like it.

I realised that our emotions are not always the best indicator of what is really happening in our lives. Mastering our emotions, therefore, is key to maintaining balance as resilient leaders. This was far from easy during the pandemic, when we all had valid reasons to feel anxious and fearful about an uncertain future. Yet, for me, the way forward was to steer away from panicking and to find a way to regulate my emotions, even though so much of what was happening was beyond my control.

It was only when I felt emotionally balanced that I could get in a frame of mind to maintain my focus and stay on track, working towards my goals.

Sometimes, setting boundaries can also mean blocking out time for specific tasks.

Lean Six Sigma

But how do you make the best use of your time when there are so many commitments you need to prioritise in terms of maintaining your focus?

With limited time available, what can you do to make the best use of your time and operate in a way that's as efficient as possible?

My go-to tool is Lean Six Sigma (LSS), an approach developed to improve processes and performance through operational efficiency while limiting wasted time and wasted resources. Developed within the corporate world, the way I've adapted LSS into a time management tool is by recognising that every process I commit to is made up of a series of tasks, and that there is both an efficient and an inefficient way of achieving my end goal.

Duplication of time and effort is a no-no – unless there is a compelling reason for duplication. Similarly, the more people that need to be consulted as part of a process, the more complex and cumbersome the process becomes, so there needs to be a compelling reason why more people have to be involved. In some circumstances, staying on task should involve more people, but only when this is a means of overall process improvement.

As LSS gives us a large box of tools and methodologies to play with, however, the options available can themselves become overwhelming. I keep things simple by returning, time and time again, to a baseline called DMAIC.

DMAIC is an acronym for Define, Measure, Analyse, Improve, and Control. I find this to be a really helpful structure that I can apply to a series of tasks I'm working through in order to achieve an end goal.

I first define the series of steps I have to take towards my end goal, then I think about how best to measure those steps, analyse their efficiency, improve their efficiency, and then control any improvements.

This is my own adaptive interpretation of DMAIC, and I've found that this framework works well in helping me maintain clarity around defining the clear steps I need to take towards achieving an end goal.

When Life Throws You A Curveball

Staying focused can be relatively straightforward when life is on an even keel, but what do you do when life throws you a curveball?

When you experience setback after setback, despite your best efforts?

When you experience a bereavement or series of personal losses?

When you develop a pressing health issue?

When your ability to focus is derailed by a change in life circumstances?

I have experienced all of the above, and as a result, I've learnt the importance of not only being kind to myself but also being flexible when it comes to the focus needed to achieve my goals.

Yes, we need to remain focused on our goals, but we must remain flexible in the methods we use to achieve them.

When we get hit by life's curveballs, seeking the counsel and support of others is invaluable, but be sure to lean on those you can trust and who genuinely have your best interests at heart. In seeking other people's counsel, remember that not everyone's opinion of you matters, and sometimes the best weight we can lose is the weight of other people's opinions!

At the end of the day, what other people think of you is none of your business. Their opinions can be fickle and can change in a heartbeat, so make sure you know who you can trust to lean on.

I've learnt the hard way to be careful who you lean on, because not everyone has your best interests at heart. As human beings, we are complex and emotionally driven creatures. All of us are prone to jealousy, envy, and resentment, and the last thing you want is to be seeking the counsel of someone who is already jealous of your achievements and feels intense resentment towards you.

So, how do you know whose counsel to seek out? How do you select your advisers?

I always like to have a structure and framework that I can apply to life's challenges, and I've found that the concept of a 'personal boardroom' has given me much-needed clarity when it comes to my team of advisers who can keep me on track. In their book, 'Who is in your Personal Boardroom? How to choose people, assign roles and have conversations with purpose', Zella King and Amanda Scott offer practical tools on how to build a network that will help you succeed.

The idea is that you need several specific types of people who will be assigned one of 12 designated roles within your own personal boardroom of advisers – the customer voice, the expert, the inspirer, the navigator, the unlocker, the sponsor, the influencer, the connector, the improver, the challenger, the nerve-giver, and the anchor.

Some individuals may play a dual role, but the premise is that you need all 12 roles covered across your personal boardroom (which can change and evolve over time, just like your why, what, and how).

Whenever I'm navigating a particularly challenging time, I find the counsel of my personal boardroom of advisers to be invaluable. These advisers have shown me how best to manage the emotional turmoil that comes with being hit with multiple curveballs in life.

Technology And Information Overload

The tech revolution has been both a gift and a curse.

Technology has created more opportunities for connectivity, making information more easily accessible than ever. During the global pandemic, office-based businesses were empowered by the use of virtual tech platforms, with Zoom, Teams, Google Meet, and other platforms enabling many businesses to keep operating.

Yet the way in which some technology is deployed has, in itself, stolen our attention and our focus. For example, the algorithms driving the content on social media sites are designed to hack our attention, getting us addicted to endlessly scrolling through social media content. This addictive behaviour is supported all the more by the advertising model adopted by most social media sites. Whilst I love watching YouTube videos and engaging on LinkedIn, I am all too aware of the need to limit my screen time – and of the negative impact that an unhealthy amount of screen time can have on my ability to focus.

This also applies to limiting my exposure to the news and the types of news stories I consume. Whether through mainstream media, podcasts, or YouTube, today's newsreels can rapidly lead you down a rabbit hole, leaving you to believe that the world is about to end and that we are constantly under a sustained level of threat. Much of this is driven by the freelance journalism model that has been adopted by most news outlets, often resulting in sensationalist headlines. Apart from the negative toll this can take on our mental health, consuming too much news serves as a distraction, making it even more challenging to stay focused.

So, a final tip from me as I close this chapter on the importance of focus is to limit and restrict your exposure to the news in order to maintain a more balanced frame of mind – one that supports your ability to focus on your goals.

CHAPTER 6

STAGE 2 - STAND OUT FROM THE CROWD

> *"What sets you apart can sometimes feel like a burden and it's not. And a lot of the time, it's what makes you great."*
>
> *- Emma Stone, American actress*

I had just finished delivering a talk to a group of young students at a large secondary school when a young lady came up to me.

She introduced herself and asked if she could speak to me privately.

She then went on to explain that she was British-Nigerian with a Nigerian name. She was already worrying about name discrimination when she started work and, therefore, wanted to legally change her name now to make it more anglicised. She explained that this had caused a major rift within her family because her parents were against the idea, concerned that their daughter was ashamed of her Nigerian heritage.

What would I advise her to do? she asked.

I always like to 'keep it real' and tell young people the reality of working within the corporate world as a Black woman. So, I told her of the profound sense of despair I'd felt when I experienced name discrimination when first trying to enter the solicitors' profession. I also told her how overcoming this, only to face several gender-based challenges after having my son Max, had been a bitter blow.

I told her how I'd kept asking myself how it was possible that having a Nigerian name could have such a high penalty attached to it, and how I'd found myself asking similar questions when it came to my gender and the 'motherhood penalty'.

The irony of these experiences is that they highlighted one very important thing:

I really did stand out – whether I liked it or not – and the sooner I accepted that, the better!

My advice to this young lady, therefore, was that she keep her name. That under no circumstances must she change it. That her name made her stand out. It made her unique.

Taking full advantage of the fact that I will always stand out became the second key stage in my journey towards becoming a resilient leader. If I was going to be so visible, I would make the most of this visibility and turn it into as many opportunities as possible.

Visibility Matters

Author, speaker, and purpose mentor, Jessica Huie, once told me that "a world of opportunity awaits the visible".

Her advice came at a critical turning point in my career both as a solicitor and a diversity campaigner. I was feeling overlooked when it came to my day job as a solicitor, and was similarly disappointed to see the lack of traction in my voluntary social diversity work.

Visibility unlocked opportunity with both.

I began to keep a log of my achievements at work and continued to update that log throughout the year. Then, when it came to my end-of-year performance discussion, I had plenty of examples of the work I'd delivered and its impact, which helped me not only stand out from the crowd but also gain promotions, pay increases, and a larger bonus. By embracing visibility, I was able to take more control of my end-of-year discussion with my manager whilst enjoying the advantages that embracing visibility brings.

At first, being thrust into the spotlight when I joined the global pharmaceutical industry as a senior leader in law felt deeply uncomfortable; I neither welcomed the attention I was getting nor sought it out. Yet this, too, became something that I not only had to accept but which I chose to take full advantage of as a diversity campaigner. Having such a high-profile day job gave me a tremendous platform from which I could advocate for much-needed change across the solicitors' profession. Shining a spotlight on that work became the secret sauce that propelled my advocacy's impact to another level.

Because You're Worth It

We can struggle with being visible for many reasons, more so if we are Black and female.

Being visible means exposing yourself to judgement and criticism.

It also comes with a significant amount of vulnerability.

You risk being personally attacked, often in circumstances where you have no right of reply.

The accusations that you are self-promoting, over-promoting, or not promoting enough will come thick and fast.

None of these experiences have been pleasant. However, at the same time, there are so many advantages to being visible that it makes the many downsides worth bearing.

What often lies at the heart of a reluctance to be more visible is a lack of self-worth. It's hard to stand out from the crowd if you genuinely question why anyone would value what you have to offer. As many of us lack the underlying confidence to embrace visibility, we shy away from it, preferring to remain in the shadows. The root causes of this are often due to a confluence of different factors; our upbringing and socio-economic background, cultural nuances, gender, race, nationality, and life experiences all play their part.

Getting to the root cause is key to tackling whatever particular barriers you have personally, and why your self-worth has been so badly affected. Fortunately, it is possible to uncover the root causes through counselling, mentoring, coaching, and other self-discovery methods.

Self-talk is another important factor to be aware of here. What are you telling yourself about you? Be careful how you're talking to yourself – because you are most definitely listening!

Whenever I find myself feeling unworthy for whatever reason, I pay close attention to what I'm telling myself about me. I will often discover, to my horror, that I am berating myself instead of building myself up with positive affirmations. Yes, we all make mistakes – none of us are perfect – but we should learn from our mistakes, forgive ourselves, and move on, instead of constantly telling ourselves off. The world can be hard enough without us making things even harder for ourselves through constant self-criticism.

We are too quick to believe the negative things about ourselves and too reluctant to embrace the positives. This needs to change. Vocalising positive affirmations (and standing in front of a mirror whilst doing so) is a really powerful tool when it comes to positive self-talk.

A little self-compassion goes a long way.

Play To Your Strengths

Do you know who you are?

What you're naturally good at?

What areas you need to improve on?

Standing out from the crowd can only happen if your answer to these questions is 'yes'.

Self-awareness is a critical building block in terms of becoming a visible and resilient leader, and the sooner you become aware of how you come across – and of the impact your behaviours can have on other people – the better.

There are a ton of self-awareness tools available out there, but one tool I return to time and again is the Myers-Briggs Type Indicator (MBTI).

Developed by mother/daughter duo Katharine Cook Briggs and Isabel Briggs Myers, MBTI was inspired by the work of Swiss psychiatrist Carl Jung. It involves answering a series of questions that result in one of 16 personality types, made up of four unique aspects of your preferences, each indicated by a letter.

The first letter is either **E** (for extraversion) or **I** (intraversion) and indicates whether or not you direct your energy by focusing on the outer or inner world.

The second letter is either **S** (for sensing) or **N** (for intuition, the letter **I** already having been used for intraversion) and indicates how you take in information – whether through using your senses or by focusing on the big picture, looking for relationships and patterns.

The third letter is either **F** (for feeling) or **T** (thinking) and relates to how you make decisions, whether through considering what's important to the people involved or by logically analysing the situation.

The final letter is **J** (judging) or **P** (perceiving) and relates to how you approach the outside world, whether in a planned manner or with a more flexible and spontaneous approach.

Discovering that I'm an **ESFJ** early on in my career was a real eye-opener! It made a lot of sense, explaining why I naturally enjoy public speaking and socialising so much, why I love having as much detailed information as possible, why I can be reactive and emotional, and why I find comfort in having a plan.

Importantly, it was only through understanding my own preferences that I was able to gain a better understanding of both myself and the way my preferences might impact other people. I was able to gain a better understanding of other people's preferences too, enhancing the overall effectiveness of my team at work. I even encouraged family members to complete their own MBTI assessment, including my son Max.

This self-awareness became an important foundation in helping me stand out from the crowd, supporting me in playing to my strengths whilst mitigating the negative impact my 'areas for improvement' may have. It also enriched my family relationships, improving our understanding of each other.

Armed with this improved self-awareness, I now had the courage to seek more regular feedback from colleagues and friends, much of which confirmed my MBTI profile. Good faith feedback – which is feedback provided by those who genuinely have your best interests at heart – is always a gift, and being open to regular feedback is an invaluable tool in becoming more self-aware.

Your Personal Brand

As I progressed in my career, it became clear that there were no other solicitors called Funke Abimbola. On top of this, I realised I had a unique set of characteristics, traits, and competencies that made me naturally stand out. It was this uniqueness that I used to develop my own personal brand.

Your unique selling point (USP) is focal to developing your personal brand and, therefore, standing out. So, what keywords would you use to summarise your USP? At various stages throughout my career, I've found myself writing a list of keywords that summarise *who I am.* From this, I developed keywords that focus on *what I do* – and I keep adapting these keywords over time:

Lawyer.

Leader.

Speaker.

Podcast host.

Author.

Pharma Exec.

Diversity Campaigner.

Mother.

Knowing *who you are* and *what you do* are the keys to unlocking the true potential of your unique, personal brand. This is all the more important when it comes to the critical role that your digital footprint, the internet, and social media play in enhancing your visibility, given the focus on keyword searches. Search engine optimisation (SEO) tends to relate to website effectiveness and how we can make it easier for customers and clients to find us as a business, but the same SEO principles apply when it comes to your digital footprint.

As a professional, you have plenty to offer the working world, so what keywords do you think would attract your next opportunity? You need to use these keywords consistently to embed your digital footprint so that others can find you and seek you out.

LinkedIn is the most important social media platform for professionals, and central to optimising your LinkedIn platform is using as many of these all-important keywords as possible throughout your profile so that you can be easily found for suitable opportunities.

But these keywords also matter outside of embedding your digital footprint.

I find myself using these keywords to introduce myself at networking events.

I rely on them every time I speak on a panel or deliver a keynote speech.

I use them to help me craft my biography when I'm judging an awards programme.

And these words have proven essential in developing my elevator pitch – the short pitch about ourselves that we should all be prepared to give to someone with whom we are looking to build a mutually beneficial business relationship.

By constantly reinforcing your use of these keyword descriptors, you are reinforcing your brand and your ability to stand out.

Your Network Is Your Net Worth

The prospect of networking fills many of us with a profound sense of terror and fear, yet it is only through networking – to effectively foster genuine connections – that we can leverage our ability to stand out from the crowd, enhancing our overall resilience as leaders.

I enjoy networking tremendously, but this was not always the case. The turning point for me was when I realised that networking isn't (or shouldn't be) about selling; it's about building relationships. People buy from people, and when you treat people like people, networking becomes so much easier.

Armed with your keyword descriptors and a strong sense of who you are, your networking becomes even more powerful, and whether you're networking in person or virtually, the same basic rules apply.

It's important to focus on making genuine connections through shared aims and interests. This makes your interaction more natural and free-flowing rather than forced and stilted. Recognise the value you bring to the table and keep that front of mind, being confident in the value you have to offer. Listen more than you talk to gain a better understanding of the person you're networking with and what makes them tick. Finally, follow up within a couple of days to continue the conversation after the event.

Standing out from the crowd requires courage and dedication.

It demands commitment and will involve you continually reinventing yourself as you develop your own personal brand.

But it is only through leveraging your personal brand that you can strike a chord with people, stirring their emotions, gaining their trust, and earning their loyalty.

And it is this commitment that serves as an essential phase on your way to becoming a resilient leader.

CHAPTER 7

STAGE 3 - KEEP LEARNING

> *"I'll always think about what I could have done better. Could I have come up on the net? Been more consistent? It's not anger. It's analysing: What can I do next time?"*

> *- Serena Williams, tennis player*

Embracing a Growth Mindset

A few years ago, my boss invited me to a meeting to explore and discuss a major problem within the business.

The company had tried several different approaches but nothing seemed to be working.

There was a significant amount of revenue at stake.

And, despite the fact that I knew very little about this particular business area, he had every confidence that I should be the one to take the lead on turning things around.

My initial reaction was utter disbelief. Surely there were others better equipped to lead on this? There were several subject matter experts within the company, so why couldn't one of them lead the initiative?

Despite my protestations, however, my boss was insistent, having every confidence that my leadership would have a positive impact.

I had several weeks to prepare for my new mission and, throughout that whole time, I was absolutely terrified. But the turning point came when I realised it would be a good learning opportunity, not just for me but for everyone else involved. This shifted my mindset completely, allowing me to adapt my approach.

As part of this approach, I was able to bring a disconnected team together, realign our purpose, encourage innovation, and develop creative, sustainable solutions. As a team, we found a positive way forward, safeguarding significant company revenue in the process. Our approach was even adopted by others within the organisation, making it a win for us all.

And it all started with me embracing the learning journey, because becoming a resilient leader means committing to lifelong learning.

World-renowned psychologist Carol Dweck introduced the concept of a 'growth mindset' in her bestselling book, 'Mindset: The New Psychology of Success'. A growth mindset is one that not only embraces a commitment to learning but also recognises that it's possible for us to develop our talents and intelligence through a mixture of dedicated focus, diligent hard work, and the ability and willingness to learn from our mistakes. This contrasts sharply with the polar opposite, a 'fixed mindset' – the belief that our abilities cannot be changed much, and are innate and fixed.

Learning from our mistakes entails being open to feedback – an essential part of having a growth mindset – but not all feedback is provided with the right motives. Therefore, we need to be able to recognise the difference between good faith and bad faith feedback.

Good and Bad Faith Feedback – What's the Difference?

Feedback is only as useful as the motive that lies behind the provision of that feedback. It needs to be provided in good faith with our best interests at heart; it shouldn't be driven by jealousy, envy, vindictiveness, or any other ulterior motives.

The difference between good and bad faith feedback was well explained by American professor and writer Brené Brown, who experienced an avalanche of bad faith feedback after a recording of one of her talks went viral. In her video, 'Why Your Critics Aren't the Ones Who Count', she explains the devastating impact this had on her at the time. The turning point for her came when she discovered Theodore Roosevelt's *'Citizenship in a Republic'* speech, finding inspiration in his words that were delivered at the Sorbonne in Paris, France, on April 23rd, 1910.

Popularly known as 'The Man In The Arena' speech, one notable part stands out when it comes to our response to bad faith feedback:

"It is not the critic who counts; not the man who points out how the strong man stumbles, or where the doer of deeds could have done them better. The credit belongs to the man who is actually in the arena, whose face is marred by dust and sweat and blood; who strives valiantly; who errs, who comes short again and again, because there is no effort without error and shortcoming; but who does actually strive to do the deeds; who knows great enthusiasms, the great devotions; who spends himself in a worthy cause; who at the best knows in the end the triumph of high achievement, and who at the worst, if he fails, at least fails while daring greatly..."

Brené Brown is firmly of the view that *"...if you're criticising from a place where you're not also putting yourself on the line, I'm not interested in your feedback,"* and I have embraced this approach as I continue to develop as a resilient leader.

Being a resilient leader takes a tremendous amount of courage. It involves what Brené Brown refers to as 'daring greatly' – the willingness to step into the arena of public opinion time and time again. That arena is full of spectators, many of whom are in the cheap seats, passing judgement and criticising those leaders who are trying their best to lead with resilience and courage. Fearmongering will often emanate from those in the cheap seats, and any feedback coming from them will, inevitably, be bad faith feedback, driven by the wrong motives. Bad feedback should be discarded in its entirety.

I have experienced both good and bad faith feedback throughout my career.

For example, I was shocked and deeply upset when a former colleague gave me feedback that I was over-promoting and self-promoting. I asked him to provide me with specific examples and he initially struggled to provide any. When he eventually found a couple of examples, none of them stacked up.

One example provided was his insistence that I had deliberately placed myself in the middle of a team photo to make myself more visible and prominent, thereby self-promoting, but this was mathematically impossible. There were six of us in the team at the time and all six of us had lined up in a row for the photo. How can anyone be in the middle of a group of six people lined up in a row?

Another example he provided was that I had featured more prominently in a company video over others who had also been filmed. We watched the video together and timed how much airtime each of us had on screen. Everyone appeared for twenty seconds each so, again, his feedback was not accurate.

When I delved deeper, it became very clear what was going on: he had noticed me more because I was the only Black leader in both the team photo and the video. I was more conspicuous and, in his mind, this meant I was promoting myself over others. He also admitted that he felt threatened by my successes, and he wondered why he hadn't been invited to take part in the company video. I recognised the jealousy underlying his feedback and, consequently, saw that this was feedback given in bad faith. Ultimately, I chose to ignore his feedback in its entirety.

Conversely, a trusted colleague provided me with feedback on a piece of writing I was publishing as part of my day job. The article would be publicised broadly, both within our organisation and externally through multiple social media channels. The subject matter of the article was important, and its specific aim was to create a rallying cry for proactive action amongst the article's readers.

When I received the mark-up of my article following my colleague's review, my initial reaction was to feel disheartened and dismayed by the number of changes. Surely I couldn't have missed the mark to this extent? But when I took the time to review his changes, they made perfect sense. The article read much better once I'd incorporated his suggestions. Important messages gained far more clarity. The layout was more impactful. I could see that he had provided the feedback openly and honestly, with my best interests at heart. He genuinely wanted my article to be widely read and to have a positive impact.

This was good faith feedback, which I took on board and wholeheartedly embraced. His feedback improved my writing and I learnt a great deal from his insights and input. Because of his feedback, I was able to adapt my approach to other pieces of writing too, including various chapters of this book. The positive impact of good faith feedback can never be underestimated, so always embrace feedback that is provided in good faith.

<u>Always be Ready!</u>

As resilient leaders who are embracing a lifelong learning journey, we need to be in a constant state of preparedness. Talent is everywhere but, sadly, opportunity is not – and you never know when opportunity will come knocking. It is essential, therefore, to always be ready and prepared to make the most of the opportunities that come your way.

After several years of working as a corporate lawyer within law firms, I wanted to move industry, specifically working as an in-house lawyer within the healthcare sector. I had no idea when the opportunity would arise but, even so, I started preparing well ahead of time. I focused on learning as much as I could about the healthcare ecosystem in its entirety, reading books and news articles and doing as much research as possible. I watched countless videos and documentaries. I kept abreast of industry trends and key developments. I developed my legal expertise within the healthcare space and started representing more clients across the healthcare sector.

Over a period of time, I was able to build a solid foundation that made me a stronger and more credible candidate for an in-house role within the sector. So, when the opportunities arose, I was ready to make the most of them, interviewing well for in-house roles within the healthcare sector which eventually led to a great job offer from a large, global pharmaceutical company.

<u>The Danger in Wrongful Assumptions</u>

A growth mindset involves challenging a lot of wrongful assumptions.

And, to successfully do this, we need to own up to and acknowledge our own biases.

I will never forget the first time I became acutely aware of my own bias. I had been invited to deliver a keynote speech at a global law firm's London office. The focus of my speech was the importance of diversity and the event was taking place during Black History Month. When the white, male global chair of the firm stood up to give the welcome address, my heart sank.

My immediate assumption was that the whole evening was nothing more than a box-ticking exercise. In that moment, the narrative running through my mind was far from kind, and it all hinged on the fact that the chair was white and male. What could he possibly know about gender diversity, race ethnicity, or social mobility? I assumed that he was born to privilege, that he came from several generations of lawyers. I was furious, in a way that was quite out of proportion with the circumstances.

Thankfully, my assumptions about the chair were completely wrong. Far from being born to privilege, the chair came from humble beginnings. He had gained a place at the local grammar school, which eventually led to him studying law at university. There were no other lawyers in his family and he had overcome significant obstacles to reach his senior position. Over the years, we went on to become good friends, partnering on a range of diversity initiatives and campaigns.

Thank goodness I didn't act on my bias when I first met him!

Our biases develop over time and can become hardwired. On any given day, we are bombarded with more information than our brains can process. Consequently, our brains begin to take shortcuts, making quick assumptions along the way. The problem with this is that we can easily act on those biases, often to the detriment of others. So, how do we interrupt and manage our biases to make sure this doesn't happen?

A few years ago, my friend Kristen Pressner delivered a TEDx Talk titled, 'Are you biased? I am', focusing on this very issue. Having recognised her own biases, she devised a simple 'anti-bias' tool called 'Flip It To Test It'. This tool entails flipping the narrative around to test whether or not your bias is at play.

Applying this to my own biased narrative when I heard the white, male chair giving his opening address at the global law firm, the question I should have asked myself was this – *would I have made the same assumptions if he had been Black and/or female?* The answer to the question is, of course, a resounding, 'No!'

So, this was a clear case of my own bias shaping wrongful assumptions. Had I asked that simple question at the time, I would have been better equipped to interrupt and manage my bias, avoiding making a wrongful assumption altogether.

Kristen Pressner's 'Flip It To Test It' tool has served me well over the years, helping me challenge my biases by simply flipping the narrative around.

✶✶✶

In order to keep learning, we need to be comfortable going back to the drawing board time and time again.

This constant learning loop can be deeply uncomfortable and feel counterintuitive, because our natural inclination – once we develop expertise in one area and become recognised for that expertise – is to rest on our laurels.

We enjoy the familiarity of being in our comfort zone. Developing knowledge in one field only to go back to square one in a new area can be hugely challenging. No one wants to have to start from scratch over and over again, and it takes humility to embrace this constant learning cycle.

Yet this learning cycle is a key stage towards your development as a resilient leader; it is only through a constant cycle of learning that you can constantly up your game. It is only through embracing stretch assignments and those things that scare you that you can develop into a resilient leader. The ability and willingness to learn from your mistakes is core to all of this, and your constant question should be, "What can I learn from this?"

Whether good or bad, there is always a lesson to be learnt from every experience.

CHAPTER 8

STAGE 4 - SUPPORT OTHERS

> *"At the end of the day, it's not about what you have or even what you've accomplished. It's about what you've done with those accomplishments. It's about who you've lifted up, who you've made better. It's about what you've given back."*
>
> *- Denzel Washington, Oscar-winning actor*

The Real Purpose of Achievement

I was elated when I received my first legal award in 2012 from the Association of Women Solicitors.

Following a rigorous nomination and interview process, I was crowned *Best In-house Woman Solicitor of the Year.*

The sense of pride and joy I felt was unparalleled, and I was happy to collect my award at a ceremony at the Law Society, surrounded by my team.

More awards and accolades would follow in quick succession, recognising both my leadership and the impact of my diversity work.

And whilst it was (and still remains) wonderful to be recognised in this way, my philosophy quickly became one of '*working for the cause and not the applause*'.

My achievements mean nothing if I don't use my own privilege to help others who are less fortunate. Without an underlying purpose or mission, winning awards and being recognised can, very quickly, become hollow and meaningless.

This brings me to stage 4 in my development as a resilient leader – supporting others.

Role Modelling and Giving Back

Whether we realise it or not, many of us are role models for someone.

This statement might come as a surprise to some of you reading this book – more so if you are still young and at school – but the reality is that there will be someone, somewhere looking to you as the example they would like to follow.

Embracing this can be a real challenge, and being a role model is certainly no mean feat.

For years, I shied away from the limelight and didn't want to have the responsibility of being a role model, much less such a visible one. Yet when I was appointed to a senior role in the world's largest biotech company, I was immediately thrust into the spotlight.

I had to quickly make a choice about how best to use my newfound platform; I chose to use my visible platform to drive positive change and positive outcomes for those who are unable to do so themselves.

At first, supporting others can seem overwhelming. Initially, I asked myself what possible difference one person could make. After all, I had a busy and demanding career to keep going, as well as a son to raise. Believe me, my excuses for being ill-equipped to support other people were endless and in plentiful supply!

But then I realised that there would always be an excuse, and with this I came to another profound realisation – *if not me, then who? If not now, then when?*

So I started my voluntary work, supporting others with baby steps.

For several years, I ran a small mentoring circle for women lawyers, doing this work 'behind the scenes'. Before long, our mentoring circle developed to include lawyers who were from other under-represented groups.

It then dawned on me that it would be worth partnering with the Law Society in some way to see what could be done through the solicitors' membership body. So, over a period of years, I partnered with numerous Law Society Presidents, raising awareness of the systemic issues and other barriers to progression that lawyers from under-represented backgrounds face on a daily basis. The Law Society's own internal diversity and inclusion team grew and expanded to cover a broad range of diversity strands, dedicating time and focus towards addressing the challenges posed by each group.

To make the best use of my limited time and resources, I partnered and collaborated with others, strategically focusing on influencing senior leadership within the top 50 UK law firms.

Soon, our collective actions began to drive measurable change across the profession, attracting the attention of the UK Central Government.

The Ministry of Justice contacted me to collaborate on a major diversity initiative within the judiciary, providing an opportunity to work alongside Elizabeth Truss MP, who was then Secretary of State for Justice.

Soon after this, I became involved in 'The Lammy Review' – chaired by David Lammy MP, Member of Parliament for Tottenham – contributing towards an independent review of the treatment of, and outcomes for, Black, Asian, and minority ethnic individuals in the Criminal Justice System.

I continued mentoring extensively and also provided free talks to school students through a national charity called Speakers For Schools. I started to realign the focus of my voluntary work around supporting young people and the next generation.

Very soon, alongside my demanding day job, my employer – who was keen to leverage the expertise I'd developed through my voluntary work – offered me a site-wide diversity leadership role.

And so the giving and supporting continued...

Setting Healthy Boundaries

Over a period of time, I began to feel really, really tired.

I was being volunteered for anything and everything involving diversity within the legal profession.

The work that had once given me so much joy began to feel like an overwhelming burden.

I started to develop an increasing sense of anger and resentment, wishing people would just leave me alone and feeling as if far too many were taking me for granted.

I felt a profound and deep-rooted sense of dread as more and more requests for help landed in my inbox, coming thick and fast, irrespective of what I might be going through at the time.

Yet I still found it impossible to say 'no', and carried on giving nonetheless.

Before long, I burnt out. It became clear that I couldn't possibly continue giving and supporting others as I had been.

The challenge with being a giver and a supporter of other people is remembering to set your own limits. Unfortunately, I learnt the hard way that there is an unlimited number of takers in life, none of whom seem to place any limits on their ability to take!

An insightful conversation with a close friend gave me the perspective I needed to set healthier boundaries. She said that I was allowing people to treat me like an 'all you can eat' buffet service when I was, in fact, *Le Gavroche* – referring to the exclusive,

London-based French restaurant founded by brothers Albert and Michel Roux.

Like with *Le Gavroche*, people needed to make their reservations with me months in advance, with me placing firm limits on how many people could reserve my time.

This illumination struck a painful chord with me at the time, whilst also reminding me of an old adage – you can't pour from an empty cup.

In order to recover from burnout, I knew I had to set more healthy boundaries around my support of other people.

I could no longer be constantly accessible and available to everyone at any time.

I had to recognise that I couldn't help everyone.

It wasn't down to me to get involved in every diversity initiative in the solicitors' profession.

I wasn't here to save the world, nor could I possibly achieve such a lofty goal.

So How Best to Support?

That's all well and good, I said to myself, but how do I decide what to do with all these requests for help?

What should my decision-making process look like with regard to prioritising these requests?

I already touched on prioritisation in Chapter 5 on *Focus,* but it is worth expanding on this theme further here, specifically within the context of decision-making around who to support.

Ever practical, I lean heavily on yet another tool when it comes to making the best decisions about requests for help; the Eisenhower Decision Matrix has proven invaluable to me when sifting through copious requests.

The concept was developed by former US President Dwight D. Eisenhower, who used it to help him prioritise and manage the plethora of high-stakes issues he was confronted with in his various leadership roles – first as US Army General, then Supreme Allied Commander of NATO Forces, and then as US President.

It is a tool that prioritises tasks based on their urgency and importance.

To use the tool, you divide tasks into four boxes:

1. The tasks you will *do* first
2. The tasks you will *schedule* for later
3. The tasks you will *delegate;* and
4. The tasks you will *delete/eliminate* (also known as *ignore!*).

As requests come in, I place each one into one of the four boxes below and treat that request accordingly. This gives me the guidance and clarity I need to decide when I can and cannot help, reducing my sense of overwhelm and relieving the burden of responsibility.

I **M** **P** **O** **R** **T** **A** **N** **T**	**DO** *Do it now.*	**DECIDE** *Schedule a time to do it.*
N **O** **T** **I** **M** **P** **O** **R** **T** **A** **N** **T**	**DELEGATE** *Who can do it for you?*	**DELETE** *Eliminate/ignore it.*

While it's important to support others, you must remember to put your own oxygen mask on first and to set healthy boundaries when doing so. An empty lantern provides no light and if you don't draw the line somewhere, others will draw that line for you.

Be especially mindful when anger and resentment build up, as these are sure signs that you are giving too much.

Self-care is the fuel that allows your light to shine brightly.

Self-care isn't a 'nice to have'; it is essential, and it's impossible to become a resilient leader without it.

In supporting others, we must be especially mindful of when we need to draw on our own support network.

We must balance supporting others with ample opportunities to recharge our own batteries.

And we must be empowered to do so without feeling guilty or selfish.

CHAPTER 9

STAGE 5 - KEEP CALM AND KEEP THE FAITH

> *"Faith is taking the first step, even when you don't see the whole staircase."*
>
> *- Martin Luther King Jr, American minister and activist*

Life's Curveballs

I will never forget the day I received that phone call.

It was the call I'd been both expecting and dreading.

I immediately recognised my stepmother's voice. She was crying on the phone and then simply said, *"Funke, he's gone!"*

It was August 2012. My wonderful father had been diagnosed with late-stage liver cancer earlier that year, completely out of the blue. We knew the prognosis was not good, so my two younger siblings,

Mo and Femi, and I travelled home to Nigeria to spend some time with him that July.

Even so, it was a massive shock to hear that my father had passed away. Returning to Nigeria for the funeral that September was surreal, and the grief continued to hit me in waves for months afterwards.

How could I have known then that the loss of my father would become part of a recurring theme of sickness and loss within our family over several years?

Two years prior to this, in 2010, my brother Femi was suddenly rushed to hospital with a major infection that took weeks to diagnose, leaving us fearing the worst. Thankfully, he recovered, but this experience shook us all to our core.

The following year, a close member of the family was diagnosed with an aggressive form of breast cancer which she fought valiantly, sadly losing her battle in 2015.

By the beginning of 2012, my father had been diagnosed with liver cancer, passing away that August.

In 2014, someone close to me at the time suffered a sudden, massive heart attack, was admitted to intensive care, and was in hospital for several weeks.

Later that same year, another close family member was diagnosed with pancreatic cancer, and 2015 saw my dear mother being diagnosed with cancer too.

And, finally, my heart was broken when one of my first cousins died in a car accident in the summer of 2017.

So yes, life has thrown many curveballs my way, not least of which was this relentless cycle of sickness and death within the family. Yet, despite all this, I knew I had to find a way to keep going, maintaining both my demanding career and my home life.

What is your Anchor?

To be a resilient leader, you need to accept the unpredictable nature of life.

You need a solid anchor to steady you when the storms of life hit – and they will hit. Unfortunately, life can be very unfair, despite your best efforts.

It was wrong and unfair that I experienced name discrimination when trying to enter the legal profession.

It was devastating to find myself facing gender-based challenges after maternity leave.

And, throughout my corporate law career, I experienced racial slurs from several clients, one of whom had a habit of blaming anything that went wrong with a corporate transaction on *"too many [plural N-word] in the kitchen!"*

There were multiple instances when clients assumed I was a secretary or a paralegal. On several occasions, despite me being an experienced senior solicitor, clients would insist on my boss leading the transaction, refusing to accept that I had the experience and competence to do so.

Sexual harassment from clients was rife, as were various forms of bullying. To this day, sexual harassment and bullying remain major issues across the legal profession, as was revealed during the International Bar Association's global 2018 survey which fed into a 2019 report, 'Us Too? Bullying and Sexual Harassment in the Legal Profession.'

As I became more senior, instead of things improving, the stakes became even higher. A recent example of this – and one of the most shocking – was when I found myself experiencing yet more racism and sexism within one of my senior leadership roles, becoming the target of a particularly vicious form of personal attack for no reason other than me being a Black woman.

I still experience the significant downsides of being an 'out of the box' candidate for various opportunities, and live with constant and regular rejection despite my competencies and capabilities.

And even now, life continues to deliver regular knocks, despite my best efforts.

When the proverbial hits the fan, it's important to have a strong belief system, and for me, that is my Christian faith. I may never fully understand why certain things have turned out the way they have, but my faith will always sustain me.

All resilient leaders need a solid belief system to see them through life's challenges, and there will be many times when you need to have that blind faith in the face of a seemingly impossible situation.

Our success as resilient leaders is based on persistence – with an element of luck. The reality is, we have to force ourselves to keep going, staying calm in the midst of challenging circumstances, even when we think we can't possibly go on.

Positive Psychology

During the first wave of the global COVID-19 pandemic, I was on study leave, working towards a postgraduate certificate at Wharton Business School. My studies focused on positive psychology, with a deep exploration of how we could apply positive psychology principles towards driving positive leadership outcomes, specifically with C-suite leaders.

Little did I know how invaluable this course of study would be in terms of developing my own resilience, and even more so as we endured a successive series of lockdowns, living through constant uncertainty as the global pandemic unfolded.

Developed by American psychologist Martin Seligman, positive psychology is the study of optimal conditions that contribute to how we function – whether as people, as groups, or as organisations. Its overall aim is to improve our quality of life.

Resilient leadership requires us to be in a constant state of optimism, and it was through studying positive psychology that I learnt that optimism is a belief system, with our thoughts very much determining what we feel and what we do.

There are certain cognitive behaviours that drive our perceptions, making us better able to identify problems, which enables good outcomes. These behaviours mean that we are more likely to see a situation as a challenge, not a threat – and, therefore, to face it head-on rather than withdraw. Identifying what we can control, influence, and leverage is key to staying optimistic as this empowers us to not only change what is changeable, but also to accept what cannot be controlled.

Stephen Covey touches on similar themes in his book, 'The 7 Habits of Highly Effective People', drawing a distinction between our Circle of Concern (those things we care about but have no control over) and our Circle of Influence (things we care about and can control or impact). Developing this cognitive shift became the foundation I needed to adapt my behaviours and approach whenever life threw me a curveball.

I became more approach-oriented – walking towards the issue and stepping in to find solutions. As part of this, I became more likely to seek information about the issue, which meant I was better informed as to what the issue entailed and more likely to ask for help in getting support through that issue. I found support was more forthcoming with this considered approach.

Another core positive psychology principle that I learnt to apply was the 3 Ps, which recognise that when we are faced with issues, they are unlikely to be personal, pervasive, and permanent. This realisation was a real eye-opener for me, and even more so in the middle of a global pandemic.

Consistency, Consistency, Consistency – and Laughter!

When a challenge hits us, our daily routine is the first thing to be impacted. This, in turn, affects sleep, with the resulting sleep deprivation making it impossible to maintain a healthy perspective. And yet it is in these very circumstances that consistency becomes critically important – consistency with daily exercise, healthy eating, and sticking to a routine.

During my darkest times, when I cannot see the wood for the trees, intense exercise has been a literal lifesaver for me. I make myself exercise, no matter how I feel emotionally, because I know I will always feel better afterwards. Exercise relieves stress and gives me much-needed clarity of thought.

Healthy eating is also key, as food regulates our moods and our overall sense of well-being far more than we can possibly imagine. This consistency promotes an overall sense of positivity within me, whilst helping me maintain my sense of humour – yet another important way that I cope with life's trials.

Laughter truly is the best tonic at times, and the ability to laugh in the middle of life's dramas has held me in good stead. When my son Max broke his dominant arm during a rugby match on his 15th birthday, there seemed little to laugh about. It was a bad break leading to a major disruption in our day-to-day lives, with weekly visits to the local fracture clinic over a six-week period. But I found myself laughing hysterically when we were, once again, in the waiting room, patiently waiting for yet another appointment with Max's orthopaedic surgeon when in walked Max's rugby coach, who had also broken his dominant arm! The whole situation just seemed so utterly ridiculous as I jokingly asked, *"Who else from the rugby team can I expect to see in here, then?"*

An Attitude of Gratitude

Life can always be better.

But, conversely, it can also always be worse.

A friend once shared a story with me about a man who felt sorry for himself because he didn't have any shoes.

Then he turned around and saw another man without any feet, and this brought his own worries into sharp perspective.

Maintaining an attitude of gratitude is critical to us as resilient leaders.

In the immediate aftermath of my father's death, gratitude was the last thing on my mind. I missed my father and found the grieving process to be unbearably painful. Yet, after a period of time, it was gratitude that saw me through.

I was grateful to have had such an incredible father who had provided so well for me and my siblings.

I was thankful for the education we had, and for the many sacrifices he had to make to give it to us.

I was thankful for my happy memories of him, which I still enjoy today.

And, more than anything, I was grateful for my father's legacy and the impact he had on other people's lives.

It was my gratitude that led to me founding a medical scholarship in memory of my father. At the time of writing, the Akindolie Medical Scholarship is in its eighth year, and over 60 UK medical students have been awarded a bursary under the scheme – with many of those students having since graduated from medical school, now working as junior doctors.

Now, every time I find myself missing my father, I look at what the scholarship scheme has achieved and it immediately changes my perspective.

Developing resilience is a journey and a constant work in progress.

As part of this journey, we begin to see that resilience not only comes from within but also from without.

This is not a solo journey that we can embark on by ourselves – we need the support of others.

We all have it within us to successfully adapt when faced with difficult or challenging situations.

Our resilience is not fixed; it can grow and develop over time.

And, finally, resilience is a muscle we can all build – so let's start building it today.

> *"Do not judge me by my success, judge me by how many times I fell down and got back up again."*
>
> ***- Nelson Mandela, former President of South Africa***

THANK YOU

> *"Life is not easy for any of us. But what of that?*
>
> *We must have perseverance and above all confidence in ourselves.*
>
> *We must believe that we are gifted for something, and that this thing must be attained."*

Madame Marie Curie, Nobel prize winner (twice)

I have so many people to thank for their support and encouragement in getting me to this stage in my life.

My wonderful parents, Dr. Frank Olufemi Akindolie (my beloved, late father) and Dr. Sarah Omodele Akindolie née Jadesimi (my darling mother).

My dear step-mum, Mrs. Iyabo Akindolie.

My family, especially my closest siblings – Dr. Omowunmi Akindolie (Mo), Dr. Olufemi Akindolie (Femi) and Yewande Akindolie.

My army of friends (and please do not be offended if your name does not appear on this list. I am blessed with more friends than I can list here!) – Bola Fadina, Tola Akerele, Teju Ademola, Alero Orimoloye, Shola Awosika, Ronke Ogunbufunmi, Dolapo Akinrele, Demola Akinrele, Mazzi Odu, Maje Ayida, Tabatha Mossman, Naomi Thompson, Jacqueline Webb, Renata Crome, Molly Scanlon, Tomas Stanton, Alex Shoobert, Alex Phipps, Natalie Queiroz, Shalom Lloyd, Christina Blacklaws, Dana Denis-Smith, Stephanie Boyce, the Newtons, the Waltons, the Boyles, the Troughtons, the Pikes and Debjani and Olivia Dey.

My son Max's au pairs during the 11 years that we needed au pairs living in with us – especially Michaela Markova ('Misa' – Max's first au pair), Veronika Babakova, Veronica Babaru and Zeynep Herring.

The teachers that have impacted my life the most – Mrs Elizabeth Laybourn, Miss Sybil Warmisham and the late Mrs Anne Upton.

All my school friends from Burgess Hill Girls School, both within the day school community and the boarding school community.

All the guests that my son, Max Abimbola, and I have interviewed for *The Power of Privilege and Allyship* podcast. Thank you for trusting us with your stories.

My male gender champions, all of whom have partnered and collaborated with me to progress gender equity including Richard Pickard, Caius Datt, Paul Christopher, John Parkinson, Adam Marshall CBE, Gus Sellitto, Chuck Stephens, Chris White, Barry

Matthews, Nicholas Cheffings, Kieran Pender, Owen Marks, Dr. Jonathan Galloway and Sean Dodsworth.

My amazing, independently sourced publishing support team - Jessica Grace Coleman, whose expertise as editor and proof-reader brought the final polish to the draft of this book; Emily Dicks and Saskia Louise Ingram, the talented photographer and make-up artist who conducted the photoshoot for this book; and Jahid Munshi, whose exceptional book formatting skills transformed the word version of this book into the format that you are reading today.

My ex-husband, Toks Abimbola – for being the best possible father to our son, Max, and an exemplary co-parent alongside me.

And last (but by no means least) to my favourite person on the planet, my dear son Max - my toughest but fairest critic, my strongest defender, the joy of my life and my reason for being.

RESOURCES

Weblinks

❖ Personal website - https://funkeabimbola.com/

❖ The Power of Privilege and Allyship Podcast
  https://thepowerofprivilegeandallyship.buzzsprout.com/

❖ Vimeo page - https://vimeo.com/user62978514

❖ LinkedIn profile -
  https://www.linkedin.com/in/funkeabimbola/

❖ Positive Psychology website – www.positivepsychology.com

Talks

❖ Funke Abimbola's TEDx Talk, *'Climbing Mountains'*
  https://www.youtube.com/watch?v=qf4rbHZdyCc

❖ Brené Brown video, *'Why Your Critics Aren't the Ones Who
  Count'* - https://www.youtube.com/watch?v=8-JXOnFOXQk

❖ Kristen Pressner's TEDx Talk, *'Are You Biased? I am'*
   https://www.youtube.com/watch?v=Bq_xYSOZrgU

Books and reports

❖ Johann Hari, *'Stolen Focus: Why You Can't Pay Attention'*

❖ Simon Sinek, *'Start With Why: How Great Leaders Inspire Everyone To Action'*

❖ Zella King and Amanda Scott, *'Who Is In Your Personal Boardroom? How to Choose People, Assign Roles and Have Conversations with Purpose'*

❖ Carol Dweck, *'Mindset: The New Psychology of Success'*

❖ International Bar Association's report, *'Us Too? Bullying and Sexual Harassment in the Legal Profession'*

❖ Stephen Covey, *'The 7 Habits of Highly Effective People'*

ABOUT THE AUTHOR

Professor Funke Abimbola MBE is a UK-based, multi-award-winning business leader whose professional experience spans over 20 years.

Her first career as a corporate lawyer in the UK led to her advising an impressive global client list – amongst which were several FTSE and NASDAQ-listed companies – for over a decade.

Funke's subsequent career as a C-suite leader within several global pharmaceutical companies saw her working as a senior leader for Roche, the world's largest biotech company.

In addition to this, Funke is globally recognised for her expertise as a diversity, equity and inclusion leader, and – in Queen Elizabeth II's June 2017 birthday honours list – she was awarded an MBE (Member of the Order of the British Empire) by the Queen for services to diversity and young people.

Both the University of Hertfordshire and the University of Kent have awarded Funke honorary doctorates to recognise the impact of her leadership, while her alma mater – Newcastle University –

appointed her as Professor of Practice due to her leadership impact and contributions.

She has extensive non-executive director experience and has served on the board of a fully listed company, as well as in other non-executive roles. A Nigerian-born naturalised Brit, Funke has dual Nigerian and British citizenship. She speaks Yoruba (a Nigerian language) fluently and is a regular commentator on BBC TV and radio.

She is the proud mother of a 21-year-old son, who is a future software engineer. Together, they host a successful global podcast series called *The Power of Privilege and Allyship*, showcasing exceptional role models who have used their privilege to maximise the impact of their allyship in order to transform lives.

At the time of publication, Funke and her son have completed six seasons of the podcast, amassing a global audience across 1,300+ cities, almost 90 countries, and all seven continents, interviewing over 100 inspiring leaders in the process. Ranked and listed on all major podcast platforms including Apple, Spotify and Google, the podcast now has over 10,000 downloads and an estimated 70,000+ listens.

Printed in Great Britain
by Amazon

33377138R00086